GW00586421

Qualifications and Credit Framework (QCF)
LEVEL 4 DIPLOMA IN ACCOUNTING

TEXT

Option Paper:
Personal Tax
FA 2012

August 2012 Edition

For assessments from 1 January 2013

First edition 2010

Fourth edition August 2012

ISBN 9781 4453 9828 0

(Previous ISBN 9781 4453 7873 2)

British Library Cataloguing-in-Publication Data
A catalogue record for this book is available from the British
Library

Published by
BPP Learning Media Ltd
BPP House
Aldine Place
London
W12 8AA

www.bpp.com/learningmedia

Printed in the United Kingdom

CONTENTS

BPP note: AAT have advised us assessments under FA 2011 will cease to be available from 31 December 2012. Assessments under FA 2012 will be available from 1 January 2013 until 31 December 2013. This Text edition includes the provisions of FA 2012. Please ensure you check the date you intend to sit your assessment to ensure you are using the correct material.

A NOTE ABOUT COPYRIGHT

BPP LEARNING MEDIA'S AAT MATERIALS

Since July 2010 the AAT's assessments have fallen within the **Qualifications and Credit Framework** and most papers are now assessed by way of an on demand **computer based assessment**. BPP Learning Media has invested heavily to ensure our ground breaking materials are as relevant as possible for this method of assessment. In particular, our **suite of online resources** ensures that you are prepared for online testing by allowing you to practise numerous online tasks that are similar to the tasks you will encounter in the AAT's assessments.

The BPP range of resources comprises:

- **Texts**, covering all the knowledge and understanding needed by students, with numerous illustrations of 'how it works', practical examples and tasks for you to use to consolidate your learning. The majority of tasks within the texts have been written in an interactive style that reflects the style of the online tasks we anticipate the AAT will set.

- **Question Banks**, including additional learning questions plus the AAT practice assessment and a number of other full practice assessments prepared by BPP Learning Media Ltd. Full answers to all questions and assessments, prepared by BPP Learning Media Ltd, are included. Our Question Banks are provided free of charge in an online environment containing tasks similar to those you will encounter in the AAT's testing environment. This means you can become familiar with being tested in an online environment prior to completing the real assessment.

- **Passcards**, which are handy pocket-sized revision tools designed to fit in a handbag or briefcase to enable you to revise anywhere at anytime. All major points are covered in the Passcards which have been designed to assist you in consolidating knowledge.

- **Workbooks**, which have been designed to cover the units that are assessed by way of project/case study. The workbooks contain many practical tasks to assist in the learning process and also a sample assessment or project to work through.

- **Lecturers' resources**, providing a further bank of tasks, answers and full practice assessments for classroom use, available separately only to lecturers whose colleges adopt BPP Learning Media material. The practice assessments within the lecturers' resources are available in both paper format and online in e format.

This Text for Personal Tax has been written specifically to ensure comprehensive yet concise coverage of the AAT's learning outcomes and assessment criteria.

Each chapter contains:

- Clear, step by step explanation of the topic

- Logical progression and linking from one chapter to the next

- Numerous illustrations of 'how it works'

- Interactive tasks within the text of the chapter itself, with answers at the back of the book. In general, these tasks have been written in the interactive form that students will see in their real assessments

- Test your learning questions of varying complexity, again with answers supplied at the back of the book. In general these test questions have been written in the interactive form that students will see in their real assessments

The emphasis in all tasks and test questions is on the practical application of the skills acquired.

If you have any comments about this book, please e-mail ambercottrell@bpp.com or write to Amber Cottrell, Tax Publishing Manager, BPP Learning Media Ltd, BPP House, Aldine Place, London W12 8AA.

ASSESSMENT STRATEGY

Personal Tax is one of two tax assessments at Level 4.

The assessment is normally a two hour computer based assessment.

The Personal Tax assessment consists of twenty-three tasks, fourteen in Section 1 and nine in Section 2.

Section 1 covers:

- General tax
- Employment income
- Investment, savings and dividend income
- Payment of tax
- Tax returns (including the property and capital gains tax supplementary pages)

Section one will have eleven objective questions, plus three requiring an extended written response.

Section 2 covers:

- Property income
- Capital gains tax

Section two will include eight objective questions, plus one requiring an extended written response.

COMPETENCY

Learners will be required to demonstrate competence in both sections of the assessment. For the purpose of assessment the competency level for AAT assessment is set at 70 per cent. The level descriptor in the table below describes the ability and skills students at this level must successfully demonstrate to achieve competence.

QCF Level descriptor	**Summary**
	Achievement at level 4 reflects the ability to identify and use relevant understanding, methods and skills to complete tasks and address problems that are well defined but complex and non-routine. It includes taking responsibility for overall courses of action as well as exercising autonomy and judgement within fairly broad parameters. It also reflects understanding of different perspectives or approaches within an area of study or work.
	Knowledge and understanding
	▪ Practical, theoretical or technical understanding to address problems that are well defined but complex and non routine
	▪ Analyse, interpret and evaluate relevant information and ideas
	▪ Be aware of the nature and approximate scope of the area of study or work
	▪ Have an informed awareness of different perspectives or approaches within the area of study or work
	Application and action
	▪ Address problems that are complex and non routine while normally fairly well defined
	▪ Identify, adapt and use appropriate methods and skills
	▪ Initiate and use appropriate investigation to inform actions
	▪ Review the effectiveness and appropriateness of methods, actions and results
	Autonomy and accountability
	▪ Take responsibility for courses of action, including where relevant, responsibility for the work of others
	▪ Exercise autonomy and judgement within broad but generally well-defined parameters

AAT UNIT GUIDE

Personal tax

Introduction

For the purpose of assessment the Principles of Personal Tax (Knowledge) and Calculating Personal Tax (Skills) will be combined. Please read this in conjunction with the standards for the unit.

The purpose of the unit

The general purpose of these units is to enable learners to understand the impact and significance of taxation on individuals. All sources of income for individuals, such as employment income, capital gains, income from land and property and investment income are covered. By studying these taxes, learners can appreciate the tax implications for their own personal situation, and that of clients.

Learning objectives

On completion of these units the learner will be able to:

- demonstrate knowledge of how income tax and capital gains tax is applied to income

- calculate income from all sources and apply relevant allowances, deductions and reliefs to prepare accurate income tax computations

- calculate the income tax liabilities of an individual

- calculate the individual liability for capital gains tax

Learning outcomes

This unit consists of 9 learning outcomes. The learner will:

(1) demonstrate an understanding of legislation and procedures relating to personal tax.

(2) understand the current taxation principles of income from employment

(3) understand the current taxation principles of savings, non savings and dividend income for an individual.

(4) understand the current taxation principles of property income for an individual.

(5) understand the current principles of basic capital gains taxation for an individual.

(6) calculate income from all sources accurately.

(7) calculate accurately the tax payable on income.

(8) account for capital gains tax correctly

(9) prepare accurate computations and complete sections of relevant tax returns.

Delivery guidance

General tax issues

This area underpins all the other specific taxation areas assessed within this unit. It should not be seen in isolation as, for instance, the Finance Act being assessed is relevant throughout the standards.

Documentation that needs to be kept by all parties is relevant here. Both the responsibilities of the taxpayer and the tax practitioner are relevant, in particular what documents need to be kept and for how long. The responsibilities of the tax practitioner are particularly important when handling client tax affairs and learners must be able to show understanding of this.

Additionally, learners will need to show understanding of the implications on taxpayers if full, accurate and timely disclosure of all tax related information is not provided to HRMC. The tax practitioner's role in this area should also be understood.

Employment income

Learners can expect questions on the differences between employment and self employment. The basis of assessment for employment income can also be expected.

Calculations of employment income, including various assessable benefits are a crucial area of these standards. However, it is also expected that students will be able to explain this income in terms of providing basic advice to tax payers. For instance, being able to explain how job related accommodation operates is as relevant as being able to compute this benefit.

In addition, the learner must be able to show understanding of the impact of exempt benefits. This should be from an operational perspective as well as giving either tax payers or companies advice on how to effectively use exempt benefits.

Excluded topics:

Calculation of car benefit where the emission figures are not given

PAYE system

Identification of P11D employees

Property income

Income from property is an important aspect of income tax, and learners must be able to show knowledge of such income from a variety of sources. Furnished and unfurnished property, rent a room schemes, furnished holiday lettings and buy-to-let investments are all assessable. Computation of both rental income and the expenses that apply is important.

In addition, learners must be able to apply the rules for any losses made arising from these sources of income.

Excluded topics:

Leases

Other income

This will mainly apply to investment income, such as bank interest, building society interest, National Savings investments, and dividends. Some exempt income, such as interest from ISA's will also need to be understood.

Excluded topics:

Junior ISAs

Child benefit

Payment of tax

Under this heading, learners will need to be able to collate all income taxable under income tax and apply the rules for different bands and rates. This includes all rates for all levels and types of income.

An understanding of the payments on account system is crucial with learners expected to answer questions that involve both the computational aspects of this payment system, and to provide explanations to clients on how they are worked out.

The impact of pension payments, both occupational and private, will need to be understood. Such knowledge will be restricted to the computational impact of these payments. In particular, the extension of the basic rate band will need to be understood. Also, learners should be able to explain the differences between occupational and private pension payments, providing basic advice to tax payers on these differences.

The impact of charity giving also needs to be understood. Giving through employment and direct Gift Aid needs to be understood, including the differences in how tax relief is obtained. Extension of the basic rate band **also** applies here.

Personal allowances must be understood, including age allowance.

In addition to this, learners need to understand the rules for penalties and interest as they apply to payment of tax, posting of tax returns and filing of incorrect tax returns. Only rules introduced in FA07 onwards are examinable.

Excluded topics:

Complexities of pension payments, such as annual allowances or lifetime allowances

Taxpayers under the age of 16

·Married couples allowances

Blind persons allowance

Rules on penalties prior to 2010/11

Complex computations such as daily interest

Capital gains tax

Learners must appreciate who and what is taxable under this heading. The impact that relationships between connected persons have on disposal of capital assets needs to be understood.

Detailed computations can be expected on chargeable assets being disposed of, including enhancement expenditure, part disposals and chattels. Learners must expect to be examined on share disposals, including matching rules, rights issues and bonus issues.

Excluded topics:

Takeovers and reorganisations

Business reliefs such as rollover, gift and entrepreneurial relief

Small part disposals of land

Small part disposals rules as applicable to rights issues

Tax returns

There are three areas where tax returns are assessable: employment income, property income and capital gains. These are expected to be completed with accuracy and completed in conjunction with the learners own figures.

chapter 1:
THE TAX FRAMEWORK

chapter coverage 📖

In this chapter we see that individuals pay income tax on their income, and capital gains tax on their chargeable gains, and that the rules governing these taxes are laid down in both Acts of Parliament and a body of law known as case law.

Finally, we consider the responsibilities that tax practitioners have to clients and HM Revenue and Customs (HMRC), including client confidentiality.

The topics covered are:

✍ Tax position of individuals

✍ Relevant legislation and guidance from HMRC

✍ Responsibilities of tax practitioners

TAX POSITION OF INDIVIDUALS

Liability to tax

Individuals must pay **income tax on their taxable income**, and **capital gains tax on any taxable gains** arising on the disposal of chargeable assets. You will study income tax in the first part of this Text, and capital gains tax in the second part.

As a general rule, income is a receipt that is expected to recur (such as employment income), whereas a gain arises on a one-off disposal of a capital asset (eg the sale for a profit of a property held as an investment).

HM Revenue and Customs

Income tax and capital gains tax are administered by **HM REVENUE AND CUSTOMS (HMRC)**.

Tax year

Individuals must prepare personal tax computations for tax years. A TAX YEAR, FISCAL YEAR or YEAR OF ASSESSMENT is the year that runs from 6 April in one year to 5 April in the next. For example, the **2012/13 tax year** runs from **6 April 2012 to 5 April 2013**. The AAT has advised that assessments from 1 January 2013 through to 31 December 2013 will be based on the tax law that applies for the 2012/13 tax year.

In some cases, HMRC sends a taxpayer a tax return to be completed each tax year. However, most taxpayers have tax deducted from income before they receive it and this tax covers their tax liability so they are not sent a tax return by HMRC. We will look at tax returns in more detail when we consider the self-assessment system later in this Text.

Records

In order to complete a tax return or to show that the correct tax has been deducted at source, the taxpayer needs to have records of the income received, tax deducted and expenses incurred. Examples of such records include:

    (a)   Employment income: money earnings received (Form P60), taxable benefits (Form P11D), invoices for allowable expenses

    (b)   Property income: tenancy agreements, receipts for rent received and expenses paid

    (c)   Savings income: statements of interest received

    (d)   Dividend income: dividend certificates

(e) Capital gains: records of acquisition costs, enhancement costs, disposal costs, disposal proceeds

(f) General: details of Gift Aid donations made and statements of pension contributions to personal pension schemes

We look at records again when we consider the different types of income and how tax is calculated later in this Text.

Retention of records

HMRC may require taxpayers and third parties such as tax practitioners to produce records relating to a taxpayer's tax affairs.

Records must be retained until the later of:

(a) One year after the 31 January following the tax year concerned

(b) Five years after 31 January following the tax year concerned if the taxpayer carries on a business (trading income) or has property income, for example from renting out a house. In this case, the taxpayer must retain all records relating to the tax year, not just those dealing with the business or letting.

We look at the retention of records again when we consider the self-assessment system later in this Text.

HOW IT WORKS

Aleesha is employed by a firm of accountants. She also receives interest on her bank account.

She must retain records relating to income taxable in 2012/13 until 31 January 2015.

Task 1

Michael lets out a house in 2012/13 so has taxable property income for this year. He also receives some dividends from a company.

What is the date until which Michael must retain all his tax records for 2012/13?

RELEVANT LEGISLATION AND GUIDANCE FROM HMRC

Statute law

Most of the rules governing income tax and capital gains tax are laid down in STATUTE LAW, which consists of Acts of Parliament.

The existing Acts are amended each year in the annual Finance Act. In general election years there may be two or more Finance Acts, for example one before and one after the election. This Text includes the provisions of the **Finance Act 2012**. This Act will be assessed from 1 January 2013.

Some tax Acts provide for the making of detailed regulations by STATUTORY INSTRUMENT (SI). An example is the regulations which set out how employers deduct tax from employees' earnings under the Pay As You Earn (PAYE) system. A SI must be laid before Parliament and will usually become law automatically within a stated period unless any objections to it are raised.

Case law

Sometimes there may be a disagreement between HMRC and a taxpayer about how the tax legislation should be interpreted. In this situation either the taxpayer or HMRC may take the case to court. Cases about tax law are heard by the Tax Tribunal in the first instance.

Cases decided by the courts provide guidance on how legislation should be interpreted, and collectively form a second source of tax law known as CASE LAW.

You will not be expected to quote the names of decided cases in your assessment but you may need to know the principle decided in a case. Where relevant this will be noted within this Text.

HMRC guidance

To help taxpayers, HMRC publishes a wide range of guidance material on how it interprets tax law. These include:

(a) Statements of practice, setting out how HMRC intend to apply the law

(b) Extra-statutory concessions, setting out circumstances in which HMRC will not apply the strict letter of the law where it would be unfair

(c) A wide range of explanatory leaflets

(d) Revenue and Customs Briefs. These give HMRC's view on specific points

(e) Internal Guidance, a series of manuals used by HMRC staff

(f) Working Together, for tax practitioners

Much of this information can be found on HMRC's website, **www.hmrc.gov.uk.**

However, none of HMRC's guidance material has the force of law. Although you may like to have a look at this website, you should find all you need for assessment purposes within this Text.

Task 2

Indicate with ticks which two of the following have the force of law

	✓
Acts of Parliament	
HMRC Statements of practice	
Statutory Instruments	
Extra statutory concessions	

RESPONSIBILITIES OF TAX PRACTITIONERS

Responsibilities to clients and HMRC

Tax practitioners have a primary responsibility to act in the best interests of their clients. However, they also have a responsibility to deal with HMRC staff in an open and constructive manner which is consistent with the law.

AAT Guidelines on Professional Ethics

The AAT publish *Guidelines on Professional Ethics,* which set out a code of fundamental ethical principles and supporting guidance. These relate to the responsibilities that tax practitioners have to clients and to HMRC.

There are five fundamental principles which AAT members must follow:

(a) **Integrity:** a member shall be straightforward and honest in all professional and business relationships

(b) **Objectivity:** a member shall not allow bias, conflict of interest or undue influence of others to override professional or business judgements

(c) **Professional competence and due care:** a member has a continuing duty to maintain professional knowledge and skill at the level required

to ensure that a client or employer receives competent professional service based on current developments in practice, legislation and techniques. A member shall act diligently and in accordance with applicable technical and professional standards when providing professional services

(d) **Confidentiality:** see further below

(e) **Professional behaviour:** a member shall comply with relevant laws and regulations and avoid conduct that brings the profession into disrepute

Confidentiality

The *Guidelines* state that an AAT member must, in accordance with the law, **respect the confidentiality of information acquired as a result of professional and business relationships**, and **not disclose any such information** to third parties without proper and specific authority **unless there is a legal or professional right or duty to disclose**. The *Guidelines* also state that confidential information acquired as a result of professional and business relationships must not be used for the personal advantage of the member or third parties.

HOW IT WORKS

You act for Sarah in relation to her tax affairs. You and Sarah have a mutual friend, Jeremy. Sarah knows that you act for Jeremy in relation to his tax affairs and Sarah asks you to tell her whether Jeremy has invested in an ISA as she is considering making a similar investment.

You must inform Sarah that, due to client confidentiality, you cannot discuss another client's affairs, even if they are friends. However, if Jeremy gives you specific authority to disclose information about his investments to Sarah, you may do so.

Task 3

Cornelius is an acquaintance of your client, Ruby, as they have similar jobs in similar sized companies. He knows that Ruby was made redundant recently. He is facing redundancy himself and would like to know how much redundancy money Ruby received so that he can compare this to the figure his company is offering him.

State how you should reply to his request for this information, clearly justifying your reply.

Disclosure of information to HMRC

There are circumstances where the law allows a breach of the duty of confidentiality. The main situation where this arises for a tax practitioner is the requirement to produce information to HMRC.

HMRC usually informally requests information and documents from taxpayers in connection with their tax affairs. If, however, a taxpayer does not co-operate fully, **HMRC can request information and documents from a third party, such as a tax practitioner, by issuing a written 'information notice'.** An information notice issued to a third party must be issued with the agreement of the taxpayer or the approval of the Tax Tribunal.

Tax practitioners cannot be asked to produce information connected with tax advice they give to a client. For example, a tax practitioner may have to produce the detailed calculations used in the preparation of the taxpayer's return, say to value an asset, but not their reasons for choosing that method of calculation.

Material error or omission in client's tax return

The *Guidelines* state that when a member learns of a material error or omission in a tax return of a prior tax year or of a failure to file a required tax return, **the member has a responsibility to advise the client of the error or omission and recommend that disclosure be made to HMRC.**

If the client, after having had a reasonable time to reflect, does not correct the error, the member should inform the client in writing that it is not possible for the member to act for them in connection with that return or other related information submitted to the authorities.

The *Guidelines* further state that a member in practice whose client refuses to make disclosure of an error or omission to HMRC, after having had notice of it and a reasonable time to reflect, is obliged to report the client's refusal and the facts surrounding it to the Money Laundering Reporting Officer (see below) within the firm, or to the appropriate authority (Serious Organised Crime Agency (SOCA) in the UK) if the member is a sole practitioner. The member must not disclose to the client or any one else that such a report has been made if the member knows or suspects that to do so would be likely to prejudice any investigation which might be conducted following the report.

We look at the penalties that may be imposed on a client who makes a material error or omission in his tax return when we consider the self-assessment system later in this Text.

Money laundering

MONEY LAUNDERING occurs when the proceeds of criminal activities are converted into assets that appear to have a non-criminal origin.

AAT members are bound by legislation to implement preventative measures and to report suspicions to the appropriate authority. Failure to follow these legislative requirements will often be a criminal offence, leading to a fine and/or imprisonment. Firms must have appropriate procedures to ensure that knowledge and suspicions of money laundering are reported to the firm's Money Laundering Reporting Officer. A sole practitioner should make a report directly to the appropriate authority such as SOCA.

CHAPTER OVERVIEW

- Individuals may have to pay income tax and/or capital gains tax

- HMRC is responsible for the administration of tax

- The tax year runs from 6 April in one year to the following 5 April

- Taxpayers must keep records of income received, tax deducted and expenses paid

- Taxpayers must keep records until the later of:

  (a) One year after the 31 January following the tax year

  (b) Five years after the 31 January following the tax year if in business or with property income

- Some of the rules governing tax are laid down in statute law, while some are laid down in case law

- HMRC provides guidance about how tax law works, for example in Statements of Practice, Extra Statutory Concessions and Revenue and Customs Briefs

- Tax practitioners have responsibilities to their clients and to HMRC

- The ethical *Guideline* of confidentiality means that a client's tax affairs should never be discussed with third parties without the client's permission

- Tax practitioners may be required to produce information to HMRC

- A tax practitioner must cease to act for a client who refuses to disclose an error or omission to HMRC, and must make a money laundering report

- Money laundering occurs when the proceeds of criminal activities are converted into assets which appear to have a non-criminal origin

Keywords

HM Revenue and Customs (HMRC) – responsible for the administration of tax

The Tax Year, **Year of Assessment or Fiscal Year** – the year that runs from 6 April in one year to 5 April in the next year. Thus the tax year 2012/13 runs from 6 April 2012 to 5 April 2013

Statute law – legislation contained in Acts of Parliament

Statutory instrument – sets out detailed regulations relating to tax as authorised in a tax Act

Case law – decisions of the courts about the interpretation of tax statutes and is also a source of tax law

Money laundering – proceeds of criminal activities converted into assets which appear to have a non-criminal origin

BPP
LEARNING MEDIA

TEST YOUR LEARNING

Test 1

Decide whether the following statement is True or False.

All taxpayers are sent a tax return each year by HM Revenue and Customs.

	✓
True	
False	

Test 2

The two sources of tax law are:

and

Test 3

When is a tax practitioner not bound by the ethical *Guidelines* of client confidentiality?

	✓
When in a social environment	
When discussing client affairs with third parties with the client's proper and specific authority	
When reading documents relating to a client's affairs in public places	
When preparing tax returns	

Test 4

Who should a sole practitioner make a report to if he suspects a client of money laundering?

	✓
HMRC	
Nearest police station	
Serious Organised Crime Agency	
Tax Tribunal	

BPP
LEARNING MEDIA

Test 5

The tax administration within the UK is undertaken by:

	✓
The Chancellor of the Exchequer	
Companies House	
HM Revenue and Customs	
Members of Parliament	

chapter 2:
EMPLOYMENT INCOME

chapter coverage 📖

In this chapter you start your studies of the calculation of employment income. We begin by considering how to decide whether an individual is employed or self-employed. We then learn about when earnings are received for tax purposes.

Next we see how to calculate the taxable value of employer-provided benefits, and consider what benefits are exempt from tax.

Then we look at some deductions that are allowable when computing taxable employment income.

We end the chapter by looking at the supplementary employment pages that must accompany an individual's income tax return form.

The topics covered are:

✍ Employment and self-employment

✍ Taxation of employment income

✍ Taxable benefits

✍ Exempt benefits

✍ Allowable deductions

✍ Employment tax page

EMPLOYMENT AND SELF-EMPLOYMENT

When someone carries out work, it is important to be able to distinguish between employment (generating employment income) and self-employment (generating trading income).

- Employment is a contract of service

- Self-employment is a contract for services

It used to be thought that the deciding factor was the degree of control exercised by one party over the other about how the work should be done. The most that can be said now, however, is that control will always have to be considered, although it can no longer be regarded as the sole determining factor; other factors that may be of importance are such matters as:

(a) Whether the worker must be offered further work, and whether he must accept the work if offered (will indicate employment if this applies);

(b) Whether the person performing the services provides his own equipment (indicates self-employment);

(c) Whether he hires his own helpers (indicates self-employment);

(d) What degree of financial risk he takes (a high risk indicates self-employment);

(e) What degree of responsibility for investment and management he has (a high degree indicates self-employment); and

(f) Whether and how far he has an opportunity of profiting from sound management in the performance of his task (indicates self-employment);

(g) Whether he can work when he chooses (indicates self-employment);

(h) Whether he is entitled to holiday and sickness pay (indicates employment);

(i) Whether he works solely for one organisation (indicates employment);

(j) The wording used in any agreement between the parties

In other words, the fundamental test to be applied is whether the person performing the services is performing them as a person in business on his own account. You may need to look at all of the above factors and form a view based on the balance of the evidence.

Task 1

Leon undertakes some work for LEO Plc. Tick whether the following factors would indicate that he has a contract of service or a contract for services:

Factor	contract of service	contract for services
Leon must accept further work if offered	☐	☐
Leon hires his own helpers	☐	☐
Leon is entitled to paid holidays	☐	☐
Leon can profit from sound management	☐	☐

TAXATION OF EMPLOYMENT INCOME

Earnings from an office or employment are taxed as employment income.

In this assessment, earnings include:

(a) Salaries, wages, bonuses, commissions, fees and tips ('money earnings')

(b) Any benefits provided by the employer ('taxable benefits')

Certain allowable deductions can be made in the calculation of taxable earnings. We look at these later in this chapter.

When are earnings received?

Earnings generally are taxed in the tax year in which they are received.

Money earnings are treated as received at the earlier of

(a) The time when payment is made; and
(b) The time when a person becomes entitled to payment of the earnings

HOW IT WORKS

Joy is employed by R plc. She is entitled to the payment of a bonus of £2,000 on 31 March 2013, although she does not receive it until 25 April 2013.

Joy will be taxed on the bonus in 2012/13 because she is entitled to payment on 31 March 2013.

Task 2

Rio is employed by BCD plc at an annual salary to 31 December 2012 of £20,000, and an annual salary to 31 December 2013 of £22,500. On 30 April 2013 he becomes entitled to and is paid a bonus of £5,000 relating to the company's profits for the year ended 31 December 2012.

Rio's earnings for 2012/13 are:

£

If the employee is a director of a company, his earnings from the company are received on the earliest of:

(a) The time when payment is made; and

(b) The time when a person becomes entitled to payment of the earnings

(c) The time when the amount is credited in the company's accounting records

(d) The end of the company's period of account (if the amount was determined by then)

(e) The time the amount is determined (if after the end of the company's period of account)

HOW IT WORKS

Matt is a director of MN Ltd. On 25 March 2013, the company determines that it will pay Matt a bonus of £10,000 in relation to its period of account ending 31 March 2013. This is credited to Matt's director's account with the company on 10 April 2013 but he is not entitled to draw it until 30 April 2013. He actually draws out the payment from his account on 6 June 2013.

Matt is treated as receiving the bonus on 31 March 2013 (the end of the company's period of account) as the amount was determined by that time.

Task 3

Rita is a director of RS Ltd. On 10 April 2013, the company determines that it will pay Rita a bonus of £15,000 in relation to its period of account ending 31 December 2012. This is credited to Rita's director's account with the company on 15 June 2013 but she is not entitled to draw it until 31 July 2013. She actually draws out the payment on 31 October 2014.

Rita receives the bonus on:

	✓
31 December 2012	
31 March 2013	
10 April 2013	
15 June 2013	
31 July 2013	
31 October 2014	

Taxable benefits are generally received when they are provided to the employee.

Deduction of income tax by employer

An employer is required to deduct income tax from employees money earnings under the Pay As You Earn (PAYE) system. The employees therefore receive money earnings net of tax. The PAYE system also deals with taxable benefits. In most cases, this means that the employees have no further tax payable or repayable.

Details of the PAYE system are not in your syllabus.

TAXABLE BENEFITS

Taxable benefits are set out in legislation called the Benefits Code. We will see below how certain benefits are taxed, however in the absence of any specific rule, the taxable benefit will be the **cost to the employer**.

Company cars

If a car is provided for **private use** by reason of a person's employment a taxable benefit arises. This is sometimes called a "company car" benefit, although the rules apply whether the employer is a company or not. Private use includes home to work travel.

The benefit is normally a **percentage of the car's list price**.

The list price for the purpose of calculating the benefit, is the sum of:

- The list price when new, including all standard accessories

- The cost of all optional extras fitted to the car before being made available to the employee (excluding mobile phones)

- The cost of all optional extras fitted later, costing at least £100

Note: Security enhancements will not count towards the list price.

The percentage (that is multiplied by the list price) is dependant on the car's CO_2 emissions rating.

- For cars which emit CO_2 of 75g/km or less the percentage is 5%

- For cars which emit CO_2 between 76g/km and 99g/km the percentage is 10%

- For cars which emit CO_2 of 100g/km or more the percentage is 11%, however this percentage increases by 1% for every additional whole 5g/km of CO_2 emissions above 100g/km, up to a maximum of 35%.

The percentages are increased by 3% for diesel cars, again up to the maximum of 35%.

You will always be given a car's CO_2 emission rate in your assessment. If this is more than 100g/km, your first step in calculating a car benefit should be to round this down to the nearest 5g/km below the actual emissions. You then need to see by how many g/km the base figure of 100g/km is exceeded. We show how this works in the following example.

HOW IT WORKS

Nigel is provided with a petrol engine car which had a list price of £22,000. The car has CO_2 emissions of 188g/km.

Nigel's taxable car benefit for 2012/13 is calculated as follows:

First, round down 188 g/km to 185 g/km.

Then calculate the amount by which the base figure is exceeded, in this case 85g/km (185 − 100).

Then divide this by 5 ie 85/5 $\qquad$ = 17.

Add this number to 11 to give a figure to be used as the percentage

ie the taxable percentage is 11% + 17% $\qquad$ = 28%

So the car benefit is £22,000 × 28% $\qquad$ = £6,160

If an employee makes a **capital contribution** towards the cost of a car, the contribution is **deducted from the list price** used for calculating the benefit, subject to a maximum deduction of £5,000.

If an employee makes a payment for the **private use of a car** such as running costs (as distinct from a capital contribution to the cost of the car), the payment is **deducted from the benefit figure** calculated.

The car benefit is pro-rated if the car is only provided for part of the year or if it is incapable of being used for 30 or more consecutive days.

HOW IT WORKS

Vicky starts her employment on 6 January 2013 and is immediately provided with a new petrol engine car with a list price of £25,000. The car was more expensive than her employer would have provided and she therefore made a capital contribution of £6,200. Vicky contributes £100 a month for being able to use the car privately. CO_2 emissions are 223g/km. Vicky's car benefit for 2012/13 is:

	£
List price	25,000
Less: capital contribution (maximum)	(5,000)
	20,000

£20,000 × 35% (W) = £7,000

	£
3/12 × £7,000	1,750
Less: contribution to running costs (£100 × 3)	(300)
Car benefit	1,450

Working

CO_2 emissions = 220 g/km (rounded down).

The amount by which the base figure is exceeded is 120 g/km (220 – 100).

120/5 = 24

Taxable percentage = 11% + 24% = 35% (maximum).

Note cars with CO_2 emissions of 220g/km or more will use the maximum 35%.

The taxable car benefit covers all expenditure by the employer on repairs, servicing, insurance, road fund licence and cleaning of the car. No additional benefit arises in respect of these items. A taxable benefit does, however, arise in respect of a chauffeur provided for private mileage. This will be based on the cost of the chauffeur.

Task 4

On 6 July 2012 Sue was provided with a new petrol driven car by her employer. The list price of the car was £10,000. The car's CO_2 emissions are 209g/km.

The taxable benefit on the provision of the car in 2012/13 is:

£ [   ]

Fuel provided for private use

If an employer pays for fuel used for private motoring in a company car, a fuel benefit arises.

The benefit is a percentage of a base figure.

- The base figure for 2012/13 is £20,200.

- The percentage is the same percentage as is used to calculate the car benefit.

No benefit arises where it can be shown that either all the fuel provided was used only for business travel or that the employee has reimbursed the whole of the expense of any fuel provided for his private use.

There is **no** reduction to the benefit if only part of the expense for private use fuel is reimbursed by the employee.

The fuel benefit is reduced if private fuel is not available for part of a tax year. However, if private fuel later becomes available again in the same tax year, there is no reduction made.

HOW IT WORKS

An employee was provided with a new petrol engine car costing £15,000 (the list price) on 6 June 2012. During 2012/13 the employer spent £900 on insurance, repairs and the vehicle licence. The firm paid for all petrol (£2,300) without reimbursement. The employee was required to pay the firm £25 per month for the private use of the car. The car has CO_2 emissions of 104g/km.

The total taxable benefit for 2012/13 in respect of the car and fuel is calculated as follows:

	£
The car was available for ten months:	
List price £15,000 × 11%	1,650
£1,650 × 10/12	1,375
Less: contribution (10 × £25)	(250)
	1,125
Fuel benefit £20,200 × 11% × 10/12	1,852
Taxable benefit	2,977

If the contribution of £25 per month had been towards the petrol, the contribution would not be deducted, making the benefit assessable £250 greater. Conversely, if the cost of private petrol was fully reimbursed by the employee then there would have been no fuel benefit at all.

Task 5

Nissar had the use of a company car throughout 2012/13. The list price of the car was £30,000. The car had a diesel engine and CO_2 emissions of 184g/km. The company provided fuel for both private and business motoring. Nissar made a contribution of £400 towards the cost of private fuel.

The total taxable benefit arising to Nissar in 2012/13 is:

£

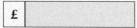

The private use of a pool car is an exempt benefit. A car is a pool car if all the following conditions are satisfied:

(a) It is used by more than one employee and is not ordinarily used by any one of them to the exclusion of the others

(b) Any private use is merely incidental to business use

(c) It is not normally kept overnight at or near the residence of an employee

Vans provided for private use

Where a van is provided to an employee that is **available for private use**, there is an **annual scale charge of £3,000.**

There is not a taxable benefit if there is no private use allowed. Private use does not include home to work travel (compare to cars where home to work travel is private use).

There is an **additional fuel benefit of £550 if fuel is provided for private use.**

Assets made available for private use

In general, if an employee uses an employer-owned asset privately (other than cars and mobile phones), an **annual benefit arises equal to 20% of the market value of the asset when first used by the employee.**

If the asset is subsequently acquired by the employee, the benefit arising on the acquisition is usually the greater of:

(a)   The market value of the asset on acquisition; and

(b)   The market value of the asset when first provided to the employee less any amounts already assessed as a benefit.

The greater of (a) or (b) is then reduced by any price paid by the employee, to give the taxable benefit.

HOW IT WORKS

A suit costing £200 is bought by an employer for use by an employee on 6 April 2011. On 6 April 2012 the suit is purchased by the employee for £15, its market value then being £25.

The taxable benefit in 2012/13 is calculated as follows:

The benefit taxable in 2011/12 will be 20% × £200 = £40

The benefit taxable in 2012/13 will be the greater of:

(a)   Market value at acquisition by employee = £25

		£	£
(b)			
	Original market value	200	
	Less: assessed in respect of use 2011/12	(40)	
		160	
	ie		160
	Less: price paid by employee		(15)
	Taxable benefit 2012/13		145

Task 6

Ahmed bought video equipment from his employer on 6 July 2012 for £1,000. The equipment was then worth £4,000. Ahmed had first used the equipment on 6 April 2011 when his employer had lent it to him for private use. Ahmed had sole use of the equipment from 6 April 2011 until he bought it on 6 July 2012. The market value of the equipment was £6,000 on 6 April 2011.

The taxable benefit for use arising in 2011/12 is:

£ ☐

and in 2012/13 is:

£ ☐

and the taxable benefit on Ahmed's acquisition in 2012/13 is:

£ ☐

Beneficial loans

Employer loans give rise to a benefit equal to:

(a) **Any amounts written-off**; and

(b) **The excess of the official rate of interest on the loan over any interest actually charged.**

There are two methods of calculating the interest benefit. **The 'average' method applies automatically unless an election is made by the taxpayer or HMRC.** (HMRC normally only make the election where it appears that the 'average' method is being deliberately exploited.)

The first method averages the balance of the loan at the beginning and end of the tax year (or the dates on which the loan was made and discharged if it was not in existence throughout the year) and applies the official rate of interest to this average. If the loan was not in existence throughout the year, only the number of complete tax months (from the sixth of the month) for which it existed are taken into account.

The second method (the alternative or 'strict' method) is to compute interest at the official rate on a daily or monthly basis on the actual amount outstanding.

BPP
LEARNING MEDIA

HOW IT WORKS

At 6 April 2012 a low interest loan of £30,000 was outstanding to a director, who repaid £20,000 on 6 December 2012. The remaining balance of £10,000 was outstanding at 5 April 2013. Interest paid during the year was £250.

The benefit under both methods for 2012/13, assuming that the official rate of interest was 4% throughout 2012/13, is calculated as follows:

Average method

	£
$4\% \times \dfrac{(30,000 + 10,000)}{2}$	800
Less: interest paid	(250)
Taxable benefit	550

Alternative method

	£
£30,000 × 8/12 x 4%	800
(6 April 2012 – 5 December 2012)	
£10,000 × 4/12 x 4%	133
(6 December 2012 – 5 April 2013)	
	933
Less: interest paid	(250)
Taxable benefit	683

Therefore the taxable benefit will be £550.

No taxable benefit arises if the combined outstanding balance on all loans to the employee did not exceed £5,000 at any time in the tax year.

When the £5,000 threshold is exceeded, a benefit arises on interest on the whole loan, not just on the excess of the loan over £5,000.

When a loan is written-off and a benefit arises, there is no £5,000 threshold: writing-off a loan of £1 gives rise to a £1 benefit.

HOW IT WORKS

Annika has two loans from her employer throughout 2012/13:

(a)   A season ticket loan of £2,300 at no interest

(b)   A loan of £24,000 at 2% interest which Annika used to buy a holiday cottage

The official rate of interest is 4%.

As the total of the loans exceeds £5,000 a taxable benefit arises in respect of both loans.

The taxable benefit that arises in respect of the loans in 2012/13 is calculated as follows:

	£
£2,300 × 4%	92
£24,000 × (4% – 2%)	480
Taxable benefit	572

Task 7

On 6 April 2012 Anton's employer provided him with an interest-free season ticket loan of £6,200. He repaid £1,000 of this loan on 6 October 2012. The official rate of interest is 4%.

The taxable benefit arising in respect of the loan in 2012/13, assuming no elections are made, is:

£ [   ]

Task 8

An employer lends an employee £4,000 to buy a car, interest-free for six months. The official rate of interest is 4%. 65% of the loan is then repaid, and the balance is written-off.

The total taxable benefit is:

£ [   ]

Accommodation

If an **employer provides an employee with accommodation**, there is a **basic benefit** equal to the higher of:

(a) The 'annual value' of the property (given in the assessment); and

(b) Any rent actually paid for the property by the employer (if the property is rented rather than owned by the employer).

The benefit is reduced by any contribution the employee makes for the use of the property.

The benefit is exempt if the accommodation is job-related.

HOW IT WORKS

Tony is provided with a company flat:

	£
Annual value	3,000
Rent paid by the company	3,380
Amount paid by Tony to the company for the use of the flat	520

Tony's taxable benefit is:

		£
Benefit: greater of:		
(a)	annual value	3,000
(b)	rent paid	3,380
ie		3,380
Less: reimbursed to the company		(520)
Net benefit		2,860

If the cost of employer-provided accommodation exceeds £75,000, an additional benefit arises. The amount of the **additional benefit** is equal to:

ORI × (C − £75,000)

- ORI is the official rate of interest at the start of the tax year. This will be given to you in the assessment, and is 4% in 2012/13.

- C is the cost of providing the accommodation. This includes the cost of purchase and the cost of any improvements made before the start of the tax year.

If the **accommodation was acquired by the employer more than six years before it was first provided to the employee**, and its original cost plus improvements exceeded £75,000, the **'cost of providing' is increased to its market value when first provided** to that employee (plus the costs of subsequent improvements before the start of the tax year).

Where any contribution paid by the employee exceeds the annual value of the property, the excess may be deducted from the additional benefit.

HOW IT WORKS

Simon's employer provided him with a house throughout 2012/13. The company bought the house for £133,000 on 1 April 2008.

For 2012/13, the annual value of the house is £1,400. Simon pays £3,000 for the use of the house to his employer.

The total benefit for 2012/13 arising in respect of the house, assuming the official rate of interest is 4% is:

Basic charge:

	£
Annual value	1,400
Less: contribution	(1,400)
	NIL

Additional charge:

	£	£
Cost	133,000	
Less:	(75,000)	
Excess		58,000
£58,000 × 4%		2,320
Less: contribution (£3,000 − 1,400)		(1,600)
Total benefit 2012/13		720

Task 9

Throughout 2012/13 Marak lived in a house provided by his employer. The following information is relevant:

Annual value	£5,200
Cost of the house (bought by employer in 2011)	£600,000
Rent paid by Marak in 2012/13	£12,000
Official rate of interest throughout 2012/13	4%

The taxable value of the accommodation provided in 2012/13 is:

	✓
£9,000	
£14,200	
£26,200	
£21,000	

Expenses connected with living accommodation

The following living expenses incurred in connection with living accommodation give rise to a taxable benefit:

(a) Heating, lighting or cleaning the premises

(b) Repairing, maintaining or decorating them

(c) Providing furniture etc normal for domestic occupation (annual value taken as 20% of cost)

If the accommodation is job-related no accommodation benefit is chargeable (see below). In that case, the maximum chargeable benefit in respect of the above expenses is 10% of the employee's net earnings, ie salary plus all other taxable benefits less any allowable deductions.

Task 10

Mr Quinton has a gross salary in 2012/13 of £27,400. He is required to live in job-related accommodation.

The annual value of the house is £2,500.

In 2012/13 the company pays an electricity bill of £550, a gas bill of £400, a gardener's bill of £750 and redecoration costs of £1,800. Mr Quinton makes a monthly contribution of £50 for his accommodation.

Mr Quinton's taxable employment income for 2012/13 is:

£ [   ]

Vouchers

An employee is normally taxable on the cost to the employer of providing a voucher exchangeable for goods or services (non cash voucher) or credit token (eg a credit card).

However, if the employee receives a voucher exchangeable for cash (cash voucher), he will be taxable on the amount for which the voucher can be exchanged.

There are some exemptions for specific vouchers. These are explained later in this chapter.

Approved mileage allowance payments

Where **employers pay mileage allowances to employees who use their own vehicles for business travel,** the employees are **taxed on any amounts received in excess** of the AUTHORISED MILEAGE RATES (AMR).

The authorised mileage rates for cars are:

- 45p a mile for the first 10,000 miles, and

- 25p a mile thereafter.

There are separate mileage rates for motorcycles and bicycles. If you need any of these rates, they will be given to you in the assessment.

If there is no allowance, or if the allowance received by the employee is less than the amount calculated using the statutory rates, the **employee may deduct the shortfall** when calculating taxable earnings.

HOW IT WORKS

Owen drives 14,000 business miles in 2012/13 using his own car.

You are required to calculate the taxable benefit/allowable deduction assuming:

    (a)   He is reimbursed 45p a mile
    (b)   He is reimbursed 25p a mile

		£
Statutory limit:	10,000 × 45p	4,500
	4,000 × 25p	1,000
		5,500

(a)

	£
Amount received (14,000 × 45p)	6,300
Less: statutory limit	(5,500)
Taxable benefit	800

(b)

	£
Amount received (14,000 × 25p)	3,500
Less: statutory limit	(5,500)
Allowable deduction	(2,000)

Task 11

Yarrik used his car to travel 12,000 business miles in 2012/13. His employer paid him 42p per business mile travelled.

The taxable benefit/ allowable deduction arising on Yarrik in respect of the amount paid to him by his employer is:

£ [   ]

Task 12

Megan uses her own car for business travel and her employer reimburses her 25p per mile. In 2012/13 Megan drove 12,000 business miles.

Megan's taxable benefit/ allowable deduction is:

£ [   ]

EXEMPT BENEFITS

There is a fairly long list of benefits that are not taxable on employees, including:

(a) **Accommodation**

Living accommodation that constitutes JOB-RELATED ACCOMMODATION. Accommodation is job-related if:

(i) Residence in the accommodation is necessary for the proper performance of the employee's duties (eg a caretaker); or

(ii) Accommodation is provided for the better performance of the employee's duties and the employment is of a kind in which it is customary for accommodation to be provided (eg a vicar or policeman); or

(iii) The accommodation is provided as part of special security arrangements in force because of a special threat to the employee's security (eg the Prime Minister).

(b) **Subsistence**

(i) Meals in a staff canteen, if they are available to all employees on broadly similar terms, and as long as there is not a contractual entitlement to receive meals instead of cash. (These would be taxable).

(ii) The first 15p per working day of meal vouchers.

(iii) Personal incidental expenses of up to £5 per night for employees working away from home in the UK, or £10 per night if working abroad that would otherwise be taxable (eg laundry, newspapers, telephone calls home).

However, where more than one night is spent away, the exemption works on an aggregate basis, eg for four nights the overall limit is £20. If the limit is exceeded, all the expenses are taxable, not just the excess.

(c) **Travel**

(i) Use of a pool car (see above).

(ii) The provision of a parking space at or near the place of work.

(iii) Approved mileage allowance payments for cars, motor bikes and bicycles within the statutory limits (authorised mileage rates) (see above).

(iv) The provision of works buses with a seating capacity of nine or more that are used mainly to bring employees to and from work.

(v) The payment of general subsidies to public bus services used by employees to travel to work.

(vi) The provision of bicycles and cycling safety equipment made available for employees mainly to travel between home and work.

(d) **Removal expenses**: up to £8,000 of removal expenses borne by the employer where the employee has to move house on first taking up the employment or on a transfer within the organisation.

(e) **Entertainment**: the provision of staff parties provided that the cost is no more than £150 per head per annum.

(f) **Childcare**: the cost of running a workplace nursery or play scheme (without limit). Otherwise up to £55 a week (for basic rate taxpayers) is tax-free if the employer contracts with an approved child carer or provides childcare vouchers to pay an approved child carer. The weekly tax-free limits for higher and additional rate taxpayers are £28 and £22 respectively. The childcare must be available to all employees and the childcare must be registered or approved home child-care.

(g) **Home-working**: a tax-free allowance of up to £4 per week is payable to employees to cover the additional household costs of working some or all of the time at home. No record keeping is required for the flat-rate allowance. For payments above that figure, evidence will be required that the payment is wholly in respect of additional household expenses incurred by the employee in carrying out their duties at home.

(h) **Work-related training and related costs**: this includes the costs of training material and assets either made during training or incorporated into something so made.

(i) **Payments by the employer to registered pension schemes**: to provide pension benefits for employees (see later in this chapter).

(j) **Miscellaneous**

    (i) Non-cash long service awards – for service in excess of 20 years, £50 per year of service is tax-free.

    (ii) Awards under a formally constituted staff suggestion scheme open to all employees on equal terms, for a suggestion outside the scope of the employee's normal duties. The award must either be not more than £25 or made after a decision is made to implement the suggestion. Awards over £25 must reflect the financial importance of the suggestion to the business. If an award exceeds £5,000, the excess over £5,000 is always taxable.

    (iii) Workplace sports or recreational facilities provided by employers for use by their staff generally. This does not apply where the employer pays or reimburses an employee's subscription to a sports club, nor where the facilities are only available to limited groups of employees.

    (iv) Air miles obtained in the course of business travel.

    (v) The private use of one mobile phone by the employee. If more than one mobile phone is provided to an employee for his private use or a phone is provided to a member of the employee's family, a taxable benefit arises based on the cost to the employer of provision of these phones.

ALLOWABLE DEDUCTIONS

The following expenditure can be deducted in the calculation of taxable earnings:

(a) Contributions to a **registered occupational pension scheme**

(b) Subscriptions to professional bodies, if relevant to the duties of employment

(c) Donations to charity under an **approved payroll deduction scheme**

(d) Qualifying travel expenses

(e) Other expenses incurred wholly, exclusively and necessarily in the performance of the duties of employment

These deductions are all made before the earnings are taxed, thereby giving tax relief at the rate applicable to the taxpayer (see later in Text).

We now look at these deductions in more detail.

Contributing to a pension

An individual may make pension provision in a number of ways.

If the individual is employed, he may join

- An **occupational pension scheme** run by his employer that is registered with HMRC and/ or

- A **personal pension scheme** run by a financial institution such as an insurance company or a bank.

If an individual is not employed, obviously he would only be able to join a personal pension scheme.

In order for a scheme to be approved or registered, it must comply with certain limits and regulations. **Tax relief is only available for contributions made to pension schemes which are registered with HMRC.**

There is a limit on the amount of contributions that an individual can make in a tax year. This limit applies to the total of all the pension arrangements that he makes, not *each* of them.

Each tax year an individual under the age of 75 may make tax-relievable pension contributions of up to the higher of:

(a)   His earnings

(b)   The basic amount (£3,600 in 2012/13)

Individuals with no earnings can, therefore, contribute £3,600 to a pension scheme each year.

Tax relief for the two schemes is quite different. Under the section 'Allowable deductions' above, this clearly refers to contributions to **occupational** pension scheme.

We will consider how tax relief is given for a personal pension scheme in chapter 5 when calculating the tax liability.

Tax relief for an occupational pension scheme

Tax relief for contributions to occupational pension schemes is usually given under NET PAY ARRANGEMENTS. This means the employer deducts the contributions from the employee's earnings before he deducts income tax under the PAYE system (as shown above as an allowable deduction).

An employer may also make contributions to a pension scheme as part of an employment benefits package. Such contributions are **exempt benefits** for the employee.

Payments from occupational pension schemes to pensioners are made after deduction of income tax under the PAYE system.

Charitable donations under payroll deduction scheme

If an employer has set up a PAYROLL DEDUCTION SCHEME, employees can make tax-deductible donations to an approved charity of their choice by asking the employer to deduct a donation from their gross earnings before deducting income tax under the PAYE system.

This method of making tax deductible donations to charity is sometimes called "Give As You Earn" or GAYE.

Qualifying travel expenses

Travel expenses are deductible if they are either incurred:

(a) On business travel, or

(b) On travelling to a TEMPORARY WORKPLACE. A workplace is temporary if the employee will return to his normal workplace at the end of a temporary period and the temporary period lasts (or is expected to last) for less than 24 months.

Travel from home to a permanent workplace is not allowable.

Approved mileage allowance payments

If an employee uses his own vehicle for business travel, the cost (to the extent that it is not reimbursed) can be claimed as a deduction, under the approved mileage allowance payments scheme (see above).

Expenses incurred wholly, exclusively and necessarily in the performance of the duties of an employment

Expenses incurred **wholly, exclusively and necessarily** in the performance of the duties of an employment are allowable deductions when calculating employment income.

Examples include travelling for business purposes, entertaining customers and subsistence costs such as meals and hotel expenses.

The test of deductibility is applied quite strictly. For example, none of the cost of renting a phone line is deductible if the phone is also used for private purposes. This is because the line is not used 'exclusively' for business purposes.

Strictly, any other expenses that have a private element are not deductible but, in practice, taxpayers are usually allowed to apportion expenses between parts that are for private purposes and those that are for business purposes. The business part of an expense is deductible.

Reimbursement of expenditure

Sometimes an employee may incur expenditure that is then reimbursed by the employer, such as business entertaining expenditure or costs of business travel, including staying in hotels. The payment by the employer will be a benefit under the Benefits Code, but the expenditure by the employee may also be an allowable deduction under the rules we have just looked at.

There are two possible treatments of the reimbursement:

(a) The employer may have agreed a **dispensation** with HMRC that the reimbursement and the expenditure by the employee will be ignored for tax purposes.

(b) In his employment pages, the employee should include the payment by the employer as a **taxable benefit** but **also** enter his expenditure as an **allowable deduction**. The two entries will cancel each other out to the extent that the expenditure is allowable.

EMPLOYMENT TAX PAGE

In your assessment you may have to complete the supplementary employment page that accompanies the income tax return form. A copy of this page is shown below.

HM Revenue & Customs

Employment
Tax year, 6 April 2012 to 5 April 2013

Your name

Your unique taxpayer reference (UTR)

Complete an *Employment* page for each employment or directorship

1 Pay from this employment - the total from your P45 or P60 - *before tax was taken off*
£

2 UK tax taken off pay in box 1
£

3 Tips and other payments not on your P60 - *read page EN 3 of the notes*
£

4 PAYE tax reference of your employer (on your P45/P60)

5 Your employer's name

6 If you were a company director, put 'X' in the box

7 And, if the company was a close company, put 'X' in the box

8 If you are a part-time teacher in England or Wales and are on the Repayment of Teachers' Loans Scheme for this employment, put 'X' in the box

Benefits from your employment - use your form P11D (or equivalent information)

9 Company cars and vans - *the total 'cash equivalent' amount*
£

10 Fuel for company cars and vans - *the total 'cash equivalent' amount*
£

11 Private medical and dental insurance - *the total 'cash equivalent' amount*
£

12 Vouchers, credit cards and excess mileage allowance
£

13 Goods and other assets provided by your employer - *the total value or amount*
£

14 Accommodation provided by your employer - *the total value or amount*
£

15 Other benefits (including interest-free and low interest loans) - *the total 'cash equivalent' amount*
£

16 Expenses payments received and balancing charges
£

Employment expenses

17 Business travel and subsistence expenses
£

18 Fixed deductions for expenses
£

19 Professional fees and subscriptions
£

20 Other expenses and capital allowances
£

ℹ️ **Shares schemes, employment lump sums, compensation, deductions and Seafarers' Earnings Deduction** are on the *Additional information* pages enclosed in the tax return pack

SA102 2010   Tax return: Employment: Page E 1   HMRC 12/09 net

HOW IT WORKS

Samantha Sing is employed by Choir plc. The following information relates to her employment:

Annual salary £35,000, with tax deducted of £5,500

Company car benefit £4,900

Fuel benefit £2,500

Private medical insurance £250

Professional subscription (paid by Samantha) £175

This would appear on the return as follows:

Name	Samantha Sing
Box 1	35000.00
Box 2	5500.00
Box 5	Choir Plc
Box 9	4900.00
Box 10	2500.00
Box 11	250.00
Box 19	175.00

CHAPTER OVERVIEW

- It is important to distinguish between income from an employment (assessable as employment income) and self-employment (assessable as trading income). The basic question is whether the person is employed under a contract of service, or performs services under a contract for services and is therefore self-employed

- An employee's earnings comprise not only his wages or salary and bonuses, but also employer-provided benefits

- Money earnings are generally received on the earlier of the time payment is made and when the employee becomes entitled to payment. There are special rules for directors

- The taxable benefit arising on a car provided for private use is a percentage of the car's list price

- For cars which emit CO_2 of 75g/km or less the percentage is 5%

- For cars which emit CO_2 between 76g/km and 99g/km the percentage is 10%

- For cars which emit CO_2 of 100g/km or more the percentage is 11%, however this percentage increases by 1% for every additional whole 5g/km of CO_2 emissions above 100g/km, up to a maximum of 35%

- The percentages are increased by 3% for diesel cars, again up to the maximum of 35%

- The private use of a pool car is an exempt benefit

- There is a taxable benefit of £3,000 a year for private use of a van (but home to work travel is not treated as private use) plus £550 if private fuel is provided

- If the employer provides the employee with assets for private use, there is a taxable benefit each year of 20% of the value of the assets when first provided

- Employer loans written-off give rise to a taxable benefit equal to the loan written-off. For a loan outstanding during the year, there is a taxable benefit equal to the excess of the official rate of interest on the loan over any interest actually charged

- The living accommodation benefit is based on the annual value of the property. An additional benefit arises where the cost of the property exceeds £75,000

CHAPTER OVERVIEW (CONTINUED)

- Expenses incurred by the employer in connection with the provision of living accommodation are fully assessable on the employee/director, unless the employee/director is in job-related accommodation. In the latter case, the maximum benefit is 10% of the net earnings from the employment

- A deduction from taxable earnings is given to employees for the cost of using their own vehicle for business travel if any mileage allowance paid is less than the statutory rates. Any excess is taxable

- There are certain exempt benefits which are not taxable on employees

- Occupational pension schemes are employer-run schemes. No taxable benefit arises in respect of employer contributions made to such schemes

- Employee contributions to an occupational pension scheme are usually deducted from the employee's taxable earnings before tax is applied

- Individuals can make pension contributions up to the higher of:
  - (a)   The basic limit (£3,600 – 2012/13)
  - (b)   Earnings

- Employees can make charitable donations under an employer's payroll deduction scheme. Such payments are deductible in arriving at taxable earnings

- Employees are generally allowed a deduction for travel costs incurred in the performance of their duties or incurred in travelling to and from a temporary workplace. Temporary is taken to be not exceeding 24 months

- For other employment-related expenses to be deductible, such expenses must be 'wholly, exclusively and necessarily' incurred 'in the performance of' the employee's duties

Keywords

The **approved mileage allowance payments scheme** – lays down authorised mileage rates (AMR) at which employees may claim an allowance for business journeys made in their own car

Job-related accommodation – accommodation that is either necessary for the proper performance of duties, is customarily provided, or is provided as part of special security arrangements

A **temporary workplace** – one at which the employee expects to be for less than 24 months

Net pay arrangements – where an employer deducts an employee's pension contributions from the employee's earnings before he deducts income tax

A **payroll deduction scheme** – set up by an employer to enable employees to make tax-deductible donations to charity

TEST YOUR LEARNING

Test 1

Someone is regarded as self-employed if he has a contract [   ], whereas if he has a contract [   ], he will be regarded as an employee.

Fill in the missing words.

Test 2

Expenses are deductible in computing taxable earnings if they are incurred [   ], [   ] and [   ] in the performance of the duties of employment.

Fill in the missing words.

Test 3

Brian uses his own car to travel 8,000 business miles in 2012/13. Brian's employer reimburses him with 35p per mile travelled. The approved mileage rate for the first 10,000 business miles travelled is 45p per mile.

The amounts that are taxable/(deductible) in calculating employment income are:

£ [   ]

Test 4

An employee is provided with a flat by his employer (not job-related accommodation). The annual value of the flat is £4,000; rent paid by the employer amounts to £5,900 per annum.

The taxable value of this benefit for 2012/13 is:

£ [   ]

Test 5

Decide whether the following statement is True or False.

A taxable fuel benefit is reduced by any reimbursement by the employee of the cost of fuel provided for private mileage.

	✓
True	
False	

Test 6

A video recorder costing £500 was made available to Gordon by his employer on 6 April 2011. On 6 April 2012, Gordon bought the recorder for £150, when its market value was £325. The assessable benefit that arises in 2012/13 is:

	✓
£325	
£400	
£175	
£250	

Test 7

Decide whether the following statement is True or False.

The first £5,000 of an interest-free loan is exempt from tax.

	✓
True	
False	

Test 8

Gautown was supplied with a petrol engine car by his employer throughout 2012/13. The list price of the car was £24,000 and its CO_2 emissions were 173 g/km.

The taxable benefit arising in respect of the car is:

£

Test 9

Buster is the Managing Director of Buster Braces Ltd and is supplied with a Bentley (three litre, petrol engine) which cost £72,000. It has CO_2 emissions of 185g/km. All running costs are borne by the company. Buster is also provided with a mobile phone for private business use. The cost of provision of the phone to Buster Braces Ltd is £750 in 2012/13.

The total taxable benefits are:

£

Test 10

For each of the following benefits, tick whether they would be taxable or exempt if received by an employee in 2012/13:

Item	Taxable	Exempt
Write off loan of £2,000 (only loan provided)	☐	☐
Payments by employer of £500 per month into registered pension scheme	☐	☐
Provision of mobile phone	☐	☐
Provision of a company car for both business and private use	☐	☐
Removal costs of £5,000	☐	☐
Accommodation provided to enable the employee to spend longer time in the office	☐	☐

chapter 3:
PROPERTY INCOME

chapter coverage 📖

In this chapter we first see what property income is and then how to compute the property income that a landlord is taxed on in a tax year. We also look at how losses on lettings are given tax relief.

We then look at the special rules that apply for qualifying holiday accommodation and renting rooms in the taxpayer's main residence (rent-a-room relief).

We end the chapter by looking at the supplementary land and property pages that must accompany the income tax return form of an individual who has let property in the tax year concerned.

The topics covered are:

✎ What is property income?

✎ Computing property income

✎ Losses

✎ Qualifying holiday accommodation

✎ Rent-a-room relief

✎ Land and Property tax form page

WHAT IS PROPERTY INCOME?

Property income is income that arises from letting out land and buildings. It can include rental income from letting out a piece of land (for example a field for grazing animals), a building such as a house, or part of a building such as a shop or a flat. The person who lets out the land or buildings is called the LANDLORD. The person who occupies the land or buildings is called the TENANT.

In the case of letting out a property in which the tenant lives, the landlord may provide furniture for the tenant to use. This is called a FURNISHED LETTING. If the tenant provides the furniture, the landlord's letting is called an UNFURNISHED LETTING. As you will see later in this chapter there are some different tax rules for furnished and unfurnished lettings.

Sometimes a taxpayer may buy a property specifically with the intention of letting it out and, possibly, benefitting from an increase in its capital value in the future. This may be called a BUY-TO-LET INVESTMENT. The same rules apply to buy-to-let investments as for any other property letting.

COMPUTING PROPERTY INCOME

Property income is taxed as non-savings income (see Chapter 4) on an ACCRUALS BASIS. The accruals basis means that all rental income **accruing in a tax year** is taxed in that year. The date that the income is actually received by the landlord is not relevant.

HOW IT WORKS

Susi bought a property on 6 September 2012. Susi began letting the property immediately for an annual rent of £36,000 payable in advance in three-monthly instalments due on 6 September, 6 December, 6 March and 6 June.

Rental income is taxed on an accruals basis. This means the income which arises from the letting for the period between 6 September 2012 and 5 April 2013 is taxed in 2012/13. Susi is therefore taxed on £36,000 × 7/12 = £21,000. She actually receives instalments of £9,000 on 6 September, 6 December and 6 March in the tax year, giving total receipts of £27,000, but this is not relevant for the tax calculation.

Expenses are also allowed on an accruals basis if they are revenue expenses (rather than capital expenses) that are **wholly and exclusively** incurred for the purpose of letting. Common allowable expenses include:

(a) Advertising for tenants, accountancy and insurance

(b) Business and water rates and council tax

(c) Bad debts if a rent payment appears unlikely to be recoverable, for example if the tenant has left the property and cannot be traced

(d) Management and agents fees

(e) Maintenance and repair costs such as redecoration

(f) Loan interest and overdraft interest if the related borrowing was applied wholly and exclusively for the purposes of letting the property

Common expenses which are not allowable include:

(a) Expenses relating to the landlord's own use of the property

(b) Capital expenses such as installing central heating, construction of walls, extensions, new ensuite bathrooms etc. The replacement of an item, such as central heating or a fitted kitchen will be treated as a repair (and so allowable) rather than a capital expense provided it is a replacement of a similar standard, not an improvement.

HOW IT WORKS

Nadine has let a property unfurnished for many years. She charged rental income of £40,000 for the year to 31 December 2012. The annual rent rose to £44,000 with effect from 1 January 2013.

Expenses relating to the letting were:

	£
Water rates (year to 31 March 2013)	2,000
Insurance (year to 31 December 2012)	600
Insurance (year to 31 December 2013)	800
Agents fees – 10% of rental income	

In June 2012 the tenant accidentally flooded the bathroom. Nadine took the opportunity to strip out the aged bathroom suite and convert the bathroom into a wet room at a total cost of £5,000. This included £900 that was the cost of repairing the flood damage.

Nadine's property income for 2012/13 is:

	£	£
Rental income		
(£40,000 × 9/12) + (£44,000 × 3/12)		41,000
Less: water rates	2,000	
insurance (£600 x 9/12) + (£800 × 3/12)	650	
agents fees	4,100	
Repairs	900	
		(7,650)
Taxable property income		33,350

Notes

The rental income and expenses must be dealt with on an accruals basis.

The cost of the flood repairs is allowable because it is a revenue expense. However, the cost of converting the bathroom into a wet room is not allowable because this is a capital expense.

Task 1

Harry owns a property that is let for ten weeks from 1 July 2012 at a rent of £160 per week. The tenants leave at the end of this period having paid only £1,300 of the total amount due. Harry writes-off the outstanding debt because the tenants cannot be traced.

The property is re-let to new tenants on 6 March 2013 for a rent of £400 per month payable in arrears (that means at the end of the month). He received the first payment on 10 April 2013.

He paid interest of £700 during the year ended 5 April 2013 on a loan to purchase the property.

Harry's taxable rental income for 2012/13 is:

£ [   ]

All letting by an individual landlord is treated as a single source of property income. This means that rents and expenses accruing in a tax year on all let properties must be pooled to arrive at a single figure for property income. The effect of this rule is that if the landlord lets several properties he can set-off the running expenses incurred on empty properties (eg properties between lets), against property income generally.

HOW IT WORKS

Bahrat lets two properties in 2012/13.

Property 1 was bought in June 2012 and let from 1 July 2012 at an annual rent of £18,000 per annum. Buildings insurance of £8,000 was paid for the year to 30 June 2013. £1,200 was spent in May 2012 on advertising for tenants.

Property 2 became vacant on 5 April 2012. Bahrat then spent £5,000 on repairing the leaking roof in the property. The property was let again with effect from 1 March 2013 for £24,000 per annum payable monthly in advance. Buildings insurance of £1,800 was incurred for the year to 31 March 2013.

Bahrat's property income for 2012/13 is:

	£	£
Rental income – property one (9/12 × £18,000)		13,500
Rental income – property two (1/12 × £24,000)		2,000
Less: buildings insurance (9/12 × £8,000)	6,000	
advertising for tenants	1,200	
Repairs	5,000	
buildings insurance	1,800	
		(14,000)
Taxable property income		1,500

Note that a loss would have arisen on property two if it had been dealt with separately. Pooling income and expenses on all let properties effectively allows a loss on one property to be set against income from other properties.

Task 2

Johnson owns two properties:

Whitehouse – let at a rental of £14,000 a year, payable quarterly in advance. The tenant was late in paying the last quarter's rent for the quarter to 5 April 2013 and Johnson did not receive payment until 25 April 2013.

Blackhouse – let at a rental of £6,800 a year payable quarterly in advance. Blackhouse was not let throughout 2012; however, a tenant moved in on 6 January 2013.

Johnson pays agents fees of 15% in respect of both properties to his managing agent. He has also incurred the following expenses:

		Whitehouse	Blackhouse
		£	£
Buildings insurance	– year to 30 June 2012	1,200	980
	– year to 30 June 2013	1,400	1,100
Advertising for tenants		–	450

Johnson's taxable property income for 2012/13 is:

£ [   ]

Depreciation on plant and machinery used in the letting business is never allowable, as capital allowances (a form of depreciation for tax purposes) are given instead. You will not be expected to compute capital allowances but you may be given a figure for capital allowances that you are expected to deduct in computing the property income.

Capital allowances are not allowed on furniture used in a property where the tenant lives. Instead, relief for such capital expenditure is given in one of two ways.

The first way is called the RENEWALS BASIS. Here the original cost of any furniture is not allowable expenditure, but the cost of replacing furniture to the same standard is allowed.

As the renewals basis is cumbersome to administer, many taxpayers use the second way, which is to claim a WEAR AND TEAR ALLOWANCE. This allowance is equal to:

10% [rents – (water rates & council tax if paid by the landlord)]

HOW IT WORKS

Polly lets out a furnished property for £8,000 a year. She pays insurance of £300 per annum and water rates of £400 per annum. Polly chooses to claim the wear and tear allowance in respect of her furniture. Polly's property income for 2012/13 is:

	£	£
Rental income		8,000
Less insurance	300	
water rates	400	
wear and tear allowance		
(10% × £(8,000 – 400)	760	
		(1,460)
Property income		6,540

Task 3

Sunita lets out a furnished property for £12,000 per annum. In 2012/13 she pays water rates of £800 and council tax of £900. She also pays an agent's fee of 10% of rent to the agent who manages the letting.

Sunita chooses to claim the wear and tear allowance in respect of her furniture.

Sunita's taxable property income for 2012/13 is:

	✓
£8,070	
£7,900	
£9,100	
£9,270	

LOSSES

If a landlord makes an overall loss from the letting of properties, **the property income in that tax year will be nil.**

The loss is carried forward and set against property income of the following year and subsequent years until the loss is completely used up.

HOW IT WORKS

Maria lets out a house at 30 Thames Drive. Her accrued income and allowable expenses are as follows:

	Income £	Expenses £
2011/12	5,000	12,000
2012/13	7,000	3,000
2013/14	15,000	6,000

The property income for Maria in all three tax years is:

£

2011/12
£(5,000 – 12,000) = £(7,000)
Taxable property income   Nil
2012/13
£(7,000 – 3,000) = £4,000 less use loss b/f of £(4,000)
Loss to c/fwd = £(7,000) - £(4,000) used = £(3,000)
Taxable property income   Nil
2013/14
£(15,000 – 6,000) = £9,000 less use rest of loss £(3,000)
Taxable property income   6,000

QUALIFYING HOLIDAY ACCOMODATION

There are special rules for the taxation of income arising from qualifying holiday accommodation. This can also be referred to as furnished holiday lettings. (FHL)

Provided certain conditions are satisfied the following special rules apply:

(a) The income qualifies as earnings for pension purposes.

(b) Capital allowances are available on furniture. The renewals basis and the wear and tear allowance do not apply if capital allowances are given.

BPP
LEARNING MEDIA

(c) Losses from furnished holiday lettings can only be carried forward against future profits from the same furnished holiday lettings business. UK losses can relieve UK furnished holiday lettings income only, and similarly with EEA losses (see below).

Qualifying holiday accommodation must be:

- Situated in the UK or elsewhere in the EEA; and

- Furnished; and

- Let on a commercial basis with a view to the realisation of profits; and

- Available for letting to the public as holiday accommodation for at least 210 days in the tax year; and

- Actually let for at least 105 days during the same tax year; and

- Not occupied for periods of 'longer-term occupation' (more than 31 consecutive days to the same person) for more than 155 days in a tax year.

Where the taxpayer also has other letting income, you must compute furnished holiday letting income separately. UK furnished holiday lettings together comprise one separate business, EEA furnished holiday lettings form another.

It is possible to aggregate the periods of actual letting of more than one property from the same qualifying business to give an average period.

The EEA is the European Economic Area and includes all the countries of the European Union (eg France, Spain) and some other European countries (eg Iceland).

Task 4

Joe owns two furnished properties in the UK that he lets out to holidaymakers during 2012/13 as follows:

	Property 1	Property 2
Available for letting	200 days	230 days
Actually let	110 days	95days

Which, if any, of his properties will qualify as furnished holiday lettings?

RENT-A-ROOM RELIEF

If an individual lets a furnished room or rooms as living accommodation in his or her main residence, then a special exemption may apply. This is called RENT-A-ROOM RELIEF. The property must have been the taxpayers main residence at some point during the tax year.

The individual may own the residence or himself rent it from a landlord. The relief can apply to lettings in a guest house provided that the house in which the business is carried on is also the taxpayer's main residence.

The limit on the relief is income from the provision of accommodation (before any expenses or capital allowances) of **£4,250 a year**. This limit is halved if any other person also receives income from renting accommodation in the property. The income to be taken into account includes charges for additional services such as laundry.

If the rental income before expenses is £4,250 or less, the rental income is wholly exempt from income tax but the expenses are ignored. However, the taxpayer may elect not to use rent-a-room relief, for example to make a loss, by taking into account both rent and expenses. It only applies for the tax year for which it is made. This election must be made by the 31 January that is 22 months from the end of the tax year concerned.

If gross rents exceed the relevant limit, the taxpayer will be taxed in the ordinary way, ignoring rent-a-room relief, unless he makes an election to use rent-a-room relief (the 'alternative basis'). If he makes the election, he will be taxable on gross receipts less £4,250 (or £2,125 if the limit is halved), with no deductions for expenses.

An election to use rent-a-room relief if gross rents exceed the limit must be made by the 31 January that is 22 months from the end of the tax year concerned. The election remains in force until it is withdrawn or until a year in which gross rents do not exceed the limit.

HOW IT WORKS

Sylvia owns a house near the sea in Norfolk. She has a spare bedroom and during 2012/13 this was let to a chef working at a nearby restaurant for £85 per week, which includes the cost of heating, lighting etc. Sylvia estimates that the extra expenses of these amount to £125 per year.

Gross rents exceeds £4,250.

Sylvia has a choice:

(1) She can be taxed on her actual profit:

	£
Rental income (£85 × 52)	4,420
Less: expenses	(125)
Taxable property income	4,295

(2) Elect for rent-a-room relief (the alternative basis): total rental income of £85 × 52 = £4,420 exceeds £4,250 limit so taxable property income is £170 (ie 4,420 – 4,250)

Sylvia should elect to use the rent-a-room basis as this will give her a lower amount of taxable property income.

Task 5

Jordan and Merry are brother and sister. They own a house jointly together and rent out one of the rooms to Zach who pays a rent of £80 per week which is split equally between Jordan and Merry. The expenses relating to the letting are £400.

Explain how Jordan and Merry will be taxed in respect of the letting to Zach.

LAND AND PROPERTY TAX FORM PAGE

In your assessment you may be asked to complete the land and property pages that must accompany the income tax return of someone who lets property. Copies of these pages are shown below.

 **HM Revenue & Customs**

UK property
Tax year 6 April 2012 to 5 April 2013

Your name	Your Unique Taxpayer Reference (UTR)

UK property details

1 Number of properties rented out

2 If all property income ceased in 2012-13 and you do not expect to receive such income in 2013-14, put 'X' in the box

3 If you have any income from property let jointly, put 'X' in the box

4 If you are claiming Rent a Room relief and your rents are £4,250 or less (or £2,125 if let jointly), put 'X' in the box

Furnished holiday lettings in the UK or European Economic Area (EEA)

Fill in one page for UK businesses and a separate page for EEA businesses. Please read pages UKPN 3 to UKPN 7 before filling in boxes 5 to 19 if you have furnished holiday lettings.

5 Income - *the amount of rent and any income for services provided to tenants*

£ . 0 0

6 Rent paid, repairs, insurance and costs of services provided - *the total amount*

£ . 0 0

7 Loan interest and other financial costs

£ . 0 0

8 Legal, management and other professional fees

£ . 0 0

9 Other allowable property expenses

£ . 0 0

10 Private use adjustment - *if expenses include any amounts for non-business purposes*

£ . 0 0

11 Balancing charges - *read page UKPN 5 of the notes*

£ . 0 0

12 Capital allowances - *read page UKPN 5 of the notes*

£ . 0 0

13 Adjusted profit for the year (if the amount in box 5 + box 10 + box 11 minus (boxes 6 to 9 + box 12) is positive)

£ . 0 0

14 Loss brought forward used against this year's profits

£ . 0 0

15 Taxable profit for the year (box 13 minus box 14)

£ . 0 0

16 Loss for the year (if the amount in boxes 6 to 9 + box 12 minus (box 5 + box 10 + box 11) is positive)

£ . 0 0

17 Total loss to carry forward

£ . 0 0

18 Put an X in the box if this business is in the EEA - *see page UKPN 6 of the notes*

19 If you want to make a period of grace election, put 'X' in the box

SA105 2012   Tax return: UK property: Page UKP 1   HMRC 12/11

Property income

Do not include furnished holiday lettings, Real Estate Investment Trust or Property Authorised Investment Funds dividends/ distributions here.

20 Total rents and other income from property

£ _____ . 0 0

21 Tax taken off any income in box 20

£ _____ . 0 0

22 Premiums for the grant of a lease – *from box E on the Working Sheet on page UKPN 8 of the notes.*

£ _____ . 0 0

23 Reverse premiums and inducements

£ _____ . 0 0

Property expenses

24 Rent, rates, insurance, ground rents etc.

£ _____ . 0 0

25 Property repairs, maintenance and renewals

£ _____ . 0 0

26 Loan interest and other financial costs

£ _____ . 0 0

27 Legal, management and other professional fees

£ _____ . 0 0

28 Costs of services provided, including wages

£ _____ . 0 0

29 Other allowable property expenses

£ _____ . 0 0

Calculating your taxable profit or loss

30 Private use adjustment – *read page UKPN 9 of the notes*

£ _____ . 0 0

31 Balancing charges – *read page UKPN 10 of the notes*

£ _____ . 0 0

32 Annual Investment Allowance

£ _____ . 0 0

33 Business Premises Renovation Allowance (Assisted Areas only) – *read page UKPN 11 of the notes*

£ _____ . 0 0

34 All other capital allowances

£ _____ . 0 0

35 Landlord's Energy Saving Allowance

£ _____ . 0 0

36 10% wear and tear allowance – *for furnished residential accommodation only*

£ _____ . 0 0

37 Rent a Room exempt amount

£ _____ . 0 0

38 Adjusted profit for the year – *from box O on the Working Sheet on page UKPN 16*

£ _____ . 0 0

39 Loss brought forward used against this year's profits

£ _____ . 0 0

40 Taxable profit for the year (box 38 minus box 39)

£ _____ . 0 0

41 Adjusted loss for the year – *from box O on the Working Sheet on page UKPN 16*

£ _____ . 0 0

42 Loss set off against 2012-13 total income – *this will be unusual - read page UKPN 15 of the notes*

£ _____ . 0 0

43 Loss to carry forward to following year, including unused losses brought forward

£ _____ . 0 0

HOW IT WORKS

Lewis Smith owns a property that he rents out throughout 2012/13 unfurnished for £600 per calendar month, payable in advance. His expenses are as follows:

Water rates £600

Electricity and gas £1,390

Mortgage interest £2,700

Insurance £500

Agent's fees £360

This would appear on the return as follows:

Page 1

Your name   Lewis Smith

Box 1   1

Page 2

Box 20   7200.00

Box 24   1100.00 (600 + 500)

Box 26   2700.00

Box 27   360.00

Box 29   1390.00

Box 38   1650.00

Box 40   1650.00

CHAPTER OVERVIEW

- Property income is income that arises from letting out land and buildings, including income from buy-to-let investments

- Property income accruing in a tax year is taxed in that year

- Property income is calculated by taking the rental income accrued and deducting allowable revenue expenditure accrued

- If an individual lets more than one property, the rents and expenses accruing on all of the let properties are pooled

- A landlord of furnished property may either use the renewals basis or the wear and tear allowance

- Rental losses must be carried forward and set against future property profits

- Income from qualifying holiday accommodation counts as earnings for pension purposes

- Capital allowances may be claimed on furniture in qualifying holiday accommodation

- Rent-a-room relief exempts up to £4,250 of property income when an individual rents a furnished room or rooms in his main residence

Keywords

Landlord – someone who rents out a property to another person called a **tenant**

Tenant – the person who occupies the land or building

Furnished letting – a letting which includes the use of furniture belonging to the landlord

Unfurnished letting – is a letting just of the property without furniture

Buy-to-let investment – a property is bought by an individual specifically with the intention of letting it out and, possibly, benefitting from an increase in its capital value in the future

Accruals basis – for taxing rental income means that all rent owing or accruing in a tax year is taxed in that year

Renewals basis – the cost of replacing furniture is allowed as an expense

Wear and tear allowance – equal to 10% (rent – water rates – council tax paid by the landlord). It may be claimed instead of the renewals basis

Qualifying holiday accommodation – furnished holiday accommodation let on commercial terms with a view to realisation of profit for a certain time each year

Rent-a-room relief – exempts all or part of the property income arising from an individual renting out part of his main residence

BPP
LEARNING MEDIA

TEST YOUR LEARNING

Test 1

David buys a property for letting on 1 August 2012 and grants a tenancy to Ethel from 1 December 2012 at £3,600 pa payable quarterly in advance.

The rental income taxable in 2012/13 is:

£

Test 2

Catherine rents out a furnished property for £16,000 pa and pays the water rates of £320 and council tax of £780 on the property.

Relief for wear and tear of furnishings is:

	✓
£1,600	
£1,490	
£1,568	
£1,522	

Test 3

John pays buildings insurance premiums for 12 months in advance on 1 October each year to cover all his letting properties. He pays £4,800 in 2011 and £5,200 in 2012.

How much would be allowed against his rental income for 2012/13?

£

Test 4

Explain how the loss arising from a FHL can be relieved?

Test 5

Where profits are being made, what is the main income tax advantage of letting qualifying holiday accommodation?

Test 6

Harry owns a property which he lets for the first time on 1 July 2012 at a rent of £4,000 per annum payable monthly in advance.

The first tenants left without notice on 28 February 2013 and the property was re-let to new tenants on 4 April 2013 at a rent of £5,000 per annum payable yearly in advance.

Harry's allowable expenditure was £1,000 in 2012/13.

What is his taxable rental income for 2012/13?

£	

Test 7

What is the maximum rental income in a tax year which is exempt from income tax under the rent-a-room scheme?

	✓
£2,125	
£4,250	
£4,500	
£8,105	

Test 8

Which TWO of the following are not advantages of a property being classed as a furnished holiday let?

	✓
Income can qualify as 'earnings' for pension purposes	
Capital allowances can be claimed on furniture	
Wear and tear allowance can be claimed on furniture	
Losses can be set against other income not just property income	

chapter 4:
TAXABLE INCOME

---

chapter coverage 📖

In this chapter we look at the three types of income: non-savings, savings and dividend income. We also consider what types of income are exempt from income tax.

We see how to compute an individual's taxable income, including how to deduct a personal allowance or age allowance, which is an amount of income that is not taxable. This enables us to compute an individual's taxable income for a tax year.

The topics covered are:

✐ Non-savings, savings and dividend income

✐ Exempt income

✐ Computation of taxable income

NON-SAVINGS, SAVINGS AND DIVIDEND INCOME

Non-savings income

NON-SAVINGS INCOME is all income other than interest and dividends. You have already met employment income and property income, which are the two main sources of non-savings income in Personal Tax. Other types of non-savings income include:

- Trading income: where an individual carries on a business as a sole trader or partner (dealt with in detail in Business Tax)

- Pension income

Savings income

SAVINGS INCOME is interest received for example from a bank or building society. This can be from an investment account or from a fixed rate savings bond.

An individual usually receives bank and building society interest net of 20% tax. This means that the bank/building society deducts 20% tax from the payment made to the individual and pays that tax to HMRC on the individual's behalf.

The bank/building society assumes the individual pays tax at 20%, which might not always be the case. Interest income can also be taxed at 10%, 40% or 50% dependant on levels of income.

Interest must be included gross in the income tax computation, to reflect the amount actually earned over the tax year. Therefore if interest is received net, it must be grossed-up before it is included in the income tax computation. For example, interest received of £80 must be grossed-up to £100 (£80 × 100/80).

The correct rate of tax can then be applied to the gross amount.

The tax already suffered on the interest income of £20 (and deducted by the bank) can be offset against the individual's income tax payable. If it exceeds the tax payable, the excess can be repaid.

We examine how to compute income tax payable in Chapter 5. In the assessment you may be given either the net or the gross amount of interest: read the question carefully. If you are given the net amount (the amount received or credited), you should gross-up the figure as shown above. However, if you are given the gross amount, include the figure you are given in the income tax computation.

Interest on loan stock from companies not listed on a stock exchange (called 'unlisted' or 'unquoted' companies) is also received net of 20% tax.

Some interest is received gross (without tax at 20% being deducted). Examples are:

- National Savings & Investments (NS&I) interest including interest from Direct Saver Accounts, Investment Accounts and Income Bonds (but not Guaranteed Income Bonds nor Guaranteed Growth Bonds (capital bonds) where tax of 20% is deducted at source)

- Interest on government securities (these are also called 'gilts')

- Interest on loan stock from companies listed on a stock exchange (called 'listed' or 'quoted' companies)

Task 1

Jesse receives building society account interest of £160 and £60 from a NS&I investment account.

The total amount of interest on which Jesse will be taxable is:

£ [   ]

DIVIDEND INCOME is dividends received from a company. **Dividends are always received net of a 10% tax credit.** This means a dividend received of £90 has a £10 tax credit, giving gross income of £100 to be included in the tax computation.

The tax credit attached to dividends cannot be repaid to non-taxpayers but it can be offset against a taxpayer's tax liability. We see how to compute a taxpayer's tax liability in Chapter 5.

Task 2

Maria receives dividends of £900 and building society interest of £1,600.

The gross amounts of dividends to be included in her income tax computation are:

£ [   ]

and the gross amounts of interest to be included in her income tax computation are:

£ [   ]

EXEMPT INCOME

Some income which would be taxable as savings or dividend income is exempt from income tax. You must not include this income in the income tax computation.

In your assessment you should always state if income is exempt. If you do not, you may not be awarded the available mark.

Individual savings account

An individual savings account (ISA) is a special tax exempt way of saving. In 2012/13 individuals can invest **£11,280** in ISAs, of which up to £5,640 can be held as cash.

Funds invested in ISAs can be used to buy stock market investments, units in unit trusts, fixed interest investments, or insurance policies. Dividends and interest received from ISAs are exempt from income tax, whether paid out to the investor or retained and reinvested within the ISA.

NS&I Savings Certificates

Savings certificates are issued by National Savings and Investments (NS&I). They may be fixed rate certificates or index linked and are for fixed terms of between two and five years. **On maturity the profit is tax exempt**. This profit is often called interest.

Task 3

Denis receives the following (cash amounts):

Dividends in ISA	£360
Savings certificates	
Interest on maturity of NS&I	£180
Interest from NatWest Bank deposit a/c	£80

The total amount taxable on Denis is:

	✓
£280	
£500	
£100	
£680	

Other exempt income

Other exempt income includes:

- Damages for personal injury or death

- Scholarships and educational grants (exempt as income of the student. If paid by a parent's employer, a scholarship may be taxable income of the parent)

- Prizes, lotto winnings, gambling winnings

- Premium Bond prizes

COMPUTATION OF TAXABLE INCOME

Computing total income

For each tax year, an individual may receive various 'components' of income. All income must be brought together in a personal tax computation and is called TOTAL INCOME.

In the personal tax computation income must be split into three types:

(a) Non-savings income
(b) Savings income
(c) Dividend income

HOW IT WORKS

In 2012/13, Margaret earns a salary of £30,000, receives gross interest of £1,000 and gross dividends of £1,000.

Her total income computation is:

	Non-savings income £	Savings income £	Dividend income £	Total £
Employment income	30,000			
Interest		1,000		
UK dividends			1,000	
Total income	30,000	1,000	1,000	32,000

Task 4

Tracey has the following types of income in 2012/13.

	£
Business income	44,000
Building society interest (gross)	2,000
Dividends (gross)	1,000
Lotto winnings	10

Using the preceding proforma as a guide, show Tracey's total income split into non-savings, savings and dividend income.

Personal allowance

All persons (including children) **who are under the age of 65 are entitled to a personal allowance (PA).** The personal allowance for 2012/13 is **£8,105,** but this is reduced for individuals whose total income exceeds £100,000.

The personal allowance (or the age allowance – see below) is deducted from total income to arrive at TAXABLE INCOME. The allowance is deducted first from non-savings income, then from savings income, and any remaining allowance from dividend income.

HOW IT WORKS

In 2012/13, Joe, who is aged 25, has trade profits of £3,000, receives bank interest of £14,000 and dividends of £450. Joe's taxable income for 2012/13 is:

	Non-savings Income £	Savings income £	Dividend income £	Total £
Trade profits	3,000			
Bank interest (× 100/80)		17,500		
Dividends (× 100/90)			500	
Total income	3,000	17,500	500	21,000
Less: personal allowance	(3,000)	(5,105)	–	(8,105)
Taxable income	–	12,395	500	12,895

Task 5

John, who is aged 46, has trade profits of £10,000 in 2012/13. He also received building society interest of £2,000, premium bond prizes of £250 and dividends of £4,500.

Show John's taxable income for 2012/13.

Total income over £100,000

If an individual's total income exceeds £100,000 the personal allowance is reduced by £1 for each £2 by which total income exceeds £100,000.

HOW IT WORKS

In 2012/13, Kelvin has gross employment income of £98,000, receives building society interest of £1,200, damages of £1,500 for personal injury following a fall and dividends of £4,500. Kelvin's taxable income for 2012/13 is:

	Non-savings income £	Savings income £	Dividend income £	Total £
Employment income	98,000			
Building society interest (× 100/80)		1,500		
Dividends (× 100/90)			5,000	
Total income	98,000	1,500	5,000	104,500
Less personal allowance (W)	(5,855)	–	–	(5,855)
Taxable income	92,145	1,500	5,000	98,645

Damages are exempt from income tax.

Working

	£
Total income	104,500
Less: income limit	(100,000)
Excess	4,500
Personal allowance	8,105
Less: half excess	(2,250)
Adjusted personal allowance	5,855

Task 6

In 2012/13, Zelda has employment income of £97,500, receives bank interest of £4,000 and dividends of £2,250.

The personal allowance that Zelda is entitled to in 2012/13 is:

£ [   ]

There is also special rule relating to the calculation of the personal allowance where the taxpayer has made

(a)   A Gift Aid donation, or

(b)   A contribution to a **personal** pension scheme

during the tax year.

The rule is that, for the purposes of comparing *total income* with the income limit of £100,000, total income is reduced by the gross amount of the Gift Aid donations and personal pension contributions. This amount is known as the *adjusted total income*.

Note that this rule **only** applies when calculating the personal allowance, we will look at how tax relief is given for these payments in more detail in Chapter 5. You may want to review this rule after studying that chapter.

HOW IT WORKS

Millie has total income of £108,500 in 2012/13. Millie also makes a personal pension contribution of £2,000 (gross) in 2012/13.

Millie's personal allowance is calculated as follows:

	£
Total income	108,500
Less: personal pension contribution	(2,000)
Adjusted total income	106,500
Less: income limit	(100,000)
Excess	6,500
Personal allowance	8,105
Less: half excess	(3,250)
Adjusted personal allowance	4,855

Task 7

Ernest has total income in 2012/13 of £109,000 and he makes a Gift Aid donation of £500 (gross) in January 2013.

Ernest is entitled to a personal allowance in 2012/13 of:

£ [   ]

Age allowance

A person aged 65–74 is entitled to an age allowance of £10,500 instead of the personal allowance of £8,105.

A person aged 75 or over receives a higher age allowance of £10,660 instead of the personal allowance of £8,105.

If the individual's total income exceeds £25,400, the age allowance is reduced by £1 for each £2 by which total income exceeds £25,400. The age allowance cannot be reduced below £8,105.

An individual is entitled to the age allowance, or higher age allowance, provided he attains the age of 65 or 75 respectively before the end of the tax year, or would have had he not died before his birthday.

The special rule which allows total income to be reduced by the gross amount of Gift Aid donations and personal pension contributions also applies in the calculation of the age allowance.

HOW IT WORKS

In 2012/13, Keith, who is aged 73, has gross pension income of £21,000, receives building society interest of £1,600, damages of £1,500 for personal injury following a fall and dividends of £3,600. Keith's taxable income for 2012/13 is:

	Non-savings Income £	Savings income £	Dividend income £	Total £
Pension income	21,000			
Building society interest (× 100/80)		2,000		
Dividends (× 100/90)			4,000	
Total income	21,000	2,000	4,000	27,000
Less age allowance (W)	(9,700)	–	–	(9,700)
Taxable income	11,300	2,000	4,000	17,300

Damages are exempt from income tax.

Working

	£
Total income	27,000
Less: income limit	(25,400)
Excess	1,600
Age allowance	10,500
Less: half excess	(800)
Adjusted age allowance	9,700

Task 8

In 2012/13, Zebedee, who is aged 80, has pension income of £20,500, receives bank interest of £2,000 and dividends of £4,500.

The age allowance that Zebedee is entitled to in 2012/13 is:

£ [_____]

Task 9

In 2012/13, Zaza, who is aged 70, has pension income of £33,500, and receives no other income.

The age allowance that Zaza is entitled to in 2012/13 is:

£ [_____]

CHAPTER OVERVIEW

- There are three types of income: non-savings, savings and dividend

- Non-savings income includes employment income, property income, trading income and pension income

- Savings income is interest

- If an individual receives interest net of 20% tax it must be grossed-up by multiplying by 100/80

- Dividends are received net of a 10% tax credit. Gross dividends up by multiplying by 100/90

- Exempt income includes income from individual savings accounts (ISAs), NS&I Savings Certificates and gambling winnings

- Tax computations must be prepared for a tax year

- All the components of an individual's income are added together to arrive at 'total income'

- Total income less the personal allowance or age allowance gives 'taxable income'

- The personal allowance is deducted first from non-savings income, then from savings income and finally from dividend income. It is reduced by £1 for every £2 that the individual's total income exceeds the income limit of £100,000

- The age allowance is given to individuals aged 65 or over at the end of the tax year. It is reduced by £1 for every £2 that the individual's total income exceeds the income limit of £25,400, but cannot be less than the personal allowance

- The total income figure for comparison to the income limit for the personal allowance and the age allowance is reduced by gross Gift Aid donations and personal pension contributions

BPP
LEARNING MEDIA

Keywords

Non-savings income – income other than interest and dividends

Savings income – interest received for example from a bank or building society

Dividend income – dividends received from a company

Total income – the total of an individual's income from all sources

Taxable income – an individual's total income minus the personal allowance or the age allowance

TEST YOUR LEARNING

Test 1

Classify the following types of income by ticking the correct box:

	Non-savings income	Savings income	Dividend income
Employment income	☐	☐	☐
Dividend received	☐	☐	☐
Property income	☐	☐	☐
Bank interest	☐	☐	☐
Pension income	☐	☐	☐
Interest on government stock	☐	☐	☐

Test 2

Insert the amounts that must be included in the personal tax computation in respect of the following:

	£
Building society interest received of £240	
Interest received on an individual savings account of £40	
Dividends received of £144	
Interest from government gilts of £350	

Test 3

In 2012/13 Joe has employment income of £30,000, receives dividends of £270 and interest of £250 on the maturity of his NS&I Savings Certificates. Use the table below to show his taxable income for 2012/13.

Test 4

Pratish receives property income of £3,000 and building society interest of £7,200 in 2012/13.

Use the table below to show his taxable income for 2012/13.

Test 5

Jesse has employment income of £110,000 in 2012/13. He also received building society interest of £4,000, a prize of £50 in an internet competition and dividends of £3,600.

Use the table below to show Jesse's taxable income for 2012/13.

Test 6

Zoreen has her 75th birthday on 10 May 2012. In 2012/13, she receives pension income of £20,380, bank interest of £4,000 and dividends of £5,400.

The age allowance available to Zoreen for 2012/13 is:

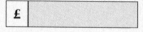

£

Test 7

Escamillo is aged 69. In 2012/13, he receives pension income of £27,500 and makes a gross gift aid donation of £1,000.

The age allowance available to Escamillo for 2012/13 is:

£

Test 8

Decide whether the following statement is True or False

The tax credit attached to a dividend can be offset against a taxpayer's tax liability, and if it exceeds the liability the taxpayer can receive a repayment.

	✓
True	
False	

chapter 5:
CALCULATION OF INCOME TAX

chapter coverage 📖

In the last chapter you saw how to compute an individual's taxable income. In this chapter you will see how to compute the income tax payable on this income.

The topics covered are:

✎ Calculating the income tax liability

✎ Calculating income tax payable

CALCULATING THE INCOME TAX LIABILITY

Income tax bands

In Chapter 4 we saw how to compute taxable income. We now see how to compute the **income tax liability** on this taxable income.

First, the taxable income needs to be divided into three bands:

(a) The first £34,370 of income; this is income in the BASIC RATE BAND

(b) The next £115,630 of income; this is income in the HIGHER RATE BAND from the higher rate threshold of £34,370 up to the ADDITIONAL RATE THRESHOLD of £150,000

(c) The remaining income; this is income in the ADDITIONAL RATE BAND which is income over the ADDITIONAL RATE THRESHOLD of £150,000

The rate of tax applied to the income in each band depends on whether the income is non-savings income, savings income or dividend income.

There is only one set of income tax bands used for all three types of income. These bands must be allocated to income in the following order:

(a) Non-savings income
(b) Savings income
(c) Dividend income

There is a special rule where the taxpayer has little or no non-savings income but has savings income. We deal with this later in this chapter.

Computing the tax liability

You need to calculate the income tax liability on taxable income as follows:

(1) Deal with non-savings income first:

- Non-savings income in the basic rate band is taxed at **20%**
- Non-savings income in the higher rate band is taxed at **40%**
- Non-savings income above the additional rate threshold is taxed at **50%**

(2) Second, deal with savings income:

If any of the basic rate band remains after taxing non-savings income it can be used here.

- Savings income that falls within the basic rate band is taxed at **20%**
- Savings income that falls within the higher rate band is taxed at **40%**
- Once savings income is above the additional rate threshold, it is taxed at **50%**.

(3) Third, compute tax on dividend income:

- If dividend income falls within the basic rate band, it is taxed at **10%** (not 20%).

- Dividend income that falls within the higher rate band is taxed at 32.5%.

- If, however, the dividend income exceeds the additional rate threshold, it is taxed at 42.5%.

(4) Total the tax = tax liability

Add the above three amounts of tax together. The resulting figure is the income tax liability.

HOW IT WORKS

Sasha has taxable income of £42,300. Of this, £32,500 is non-savings income, £6,000 is savings income and £3,800 is dividend income.

The non-savings income of £32,500 is all in the basic rate band. £1,870 of the interest uses the remaining basic rate band. £4,130 of interest and all the dividends are above the higher rate threshold of £34,370.

The tax liability is:

		Income tax
		£
(1)	**Non-savings income**	
	£32,500 × 20%	6,500.00
(2)	**Savings income**	
	£1,870 × 20%	374.00
	£34,370	
	£4,130 × 40%	1,652.00
(3)	**Dividend income**	
	£3,800 × 32.5%	1,235.00
	£42,300	
(4)	**Tax liability**	9,761

Task 1

Talet has taxable income of £60,000 for 2012/13. £25,000 of her taxable income is non-savings income. The remaining £35,000 is savings income.

Her income tax liability is:

£ _____

HOW IT WORKS

Nathan has taxable income of £185,000. Of this, £120,000 is non-savings income, £40,000 is savings income and £25,000 is dividend income.

The non-savings income of £120,000 uses all the basic rate band of £34,370 and £85,630 of the higher rate band. £30,000 of the interest uses the remaining higher rate band. £10,000 of interest and all the dividends are above the additional rate threshold of £150,000.

The tax liability is:

		Income tax £
(1)	**Non-savings income**	
	£34,370 × 20%	6,874.00
	£85,630 × 40%	34,252.00
(2)	**Savings income**	
	£30,000 × 40%	12,000.00
	£150,000	
	£10,000 × 50%	5,000.00
(3)	**Dividend income**	
	£25,000 × 42.5%	10,625.00
	£185,000	
(4)	**Tax liability**	68,751.00

Task 2

Stacey has total taxable income of £175,000 for 2012/13. Of this £120,000 is non-savings income and £55,000 is dividend income.

Stacey's income tax liability is:

£ [   ]

Savings income starting rate

There is a special rule where the taxpayer has little or no non-savings income but has savings income.

In this case, **there is a starting rate of 10% for the first £2,710 of savings income.** This is called the SAVINGS INCOME STARTING RATE BAND.

The savings income starting rate only applies where savings income falls within the savings income starting rate band. Remember that income tax is charged first on non-savings income. In most cases, an individual's non-savings income will exceed the savings income starting rate band, which will mean that savings income will fall in the basic rate band.

However, if an individual's non-savings income does not use up the savings income starting rate band of £2,710, then savings income will be taxable at the 10% savings income starting rate within that band.

HOW IT WORKS

Tamara has taxable income of £10,000 in 2012/13. £2,000 is non-savings income and £8,000 is savings income. Her income tax liability is:

	Income tax £
Non-savings income	
£2,000 × 20%	400.00
Savings income	
£(2,710 – 2,000) = £710 × 10%	71.00
£(8,000 – 710) = £7,290 × 20%	1,458.00
Income tax liability	1,929.00

Task 3

In 2012/13, Joe earns a salary of £9,000 from a part-time job and receives bank interest of £4,000.

Joe's income tax liability for 2012/13 is:

£ [   ]

Extending the basic rate band

We have seen above that an individual normally has a basic rate band of £34,370 in 2012/13. There are two circumstances in which the basic rate band must be increased. These are when the individual pays:

(a) A **Gift Aid donation**, or
(b) A contribution to a **personal pension scheme**

A Gift Aid donation is a particular type of donation to charity on which tax relief is available.

Tax relief for personal pension contributions and Gift Aid donations

We saw in Chapter 2 that if an individual is employed and makes contributions into an employer's occupational pension scheme, tax relief is obtained by the employer deducting the contribution from the employee's earnings before being taxed. In essence this means the employer administers the pension and tax relief is automatically given at the rate applicable to the individual.

For example if an individual had a salary of £100,000, and paid £10,000 into an occupational pension scheme, this would be deducted from the salary, leaving only £90,000 to pay tax on. This £10,000 would have been taxed at the higher rate of 40%, therefore the individual receives tax relief at 40% on the contribution.

An individual who pays into a **personal pension scheme** will also be entitled to tax relief at his applicable rate.

▪ **Basic rate tax relief is obtained by paying the contribution net of 20%** tax, thereby obtaining basic rate relief at the point of payment.

▪ **Higher or additional rate relief is obtained by extending the basic rate band.**

Both Gift Aid donations and contributions to personal pension schemes are paid net of 20% tax. For example, if an individual pays a pension contribution of £800, the gross amount of the donation is £800 × 100/80 = £1,000 (the individual contributes £800 into his scheme, and the government pays the £200).

If the individual is a basic rate taxpayer, no further adjustments need to be made.

If the taxpayer is liable to tax at the higher **or additional** rate, further relief is given. However, this must take account of the fact that basic rate relief has already been given. This is done by **extending the basic rate band by the gross amount of a Gift Aid donation and/or the gross amount of any personal pension contribution paid**. This means that the gross payment will be taxed at the basic rate not the higher rate.

HOW IT WORKS

Gustav has taxable income (all non-savings) of £50,000 in 2012/13.

Assuming that Gustav does not make any Gift Aid donations nor personal pension contributions in 2012/13, his income tax liability will be:

	£
£34,370 × 20%	6,874.00
£15,630 × 40%	6,252.00
£50,000	13,126.00

Now think about the situation where Gustav makes a Gift Aid donation of £8,000 in 2012/13. The Gift Aid donation will have been paid net of 20% tax. This means that the gross amount of the payment is £8,000 × 100/80 = £10,000 and Gustav's basic rate band must be extended by £10,000. His income tax liability is calculated as follows:

	£
£34,370 × 20%	6,874.00
£10,000 (extended basic rate band) × 20%	2,000.00
£5,630 × 40%	2,252.00
£50,000	11,126.00

The difference between the tax liabilities without and with the Gift Aid donation is £10,000 × (40 − 20)% = £2,000. The total tax relief is:

	£
Basic rate relief given by net payment	2,000.00
Higher rate relief given by extending basic rate band	2,000.00
Total tax relief	4,000.00

Task 4

In 2012/13 Hans has taxable income of £50,000. £24,000 of this income is non-savings income, the rest is savings income. Hans pays a personal pension contribution of £5,600 in 2012/13.

Hans' tax liability for 2012/13 is:

£ [   ]

If the taxpayer is liable to tax at the additional rate, extra relief is given. The higher rate band remains equal to £115,630. Extending the basic rate band therefore pushes the additional rate threshold up by the same amount so that the gross payment is taxed at the basic rate but not at the additional rate.

HOW IT WORKS

Lara has taxable income (all non-savings) of £180,000 in 2012/13.

Assuming that Lara does not make any Gift Aid donations nor personal pension contributions in 2012/13, her income tax liability will be:

	£
£34,370 × 20%	6,874.00
£115,630 × 40%	46,252.00
£30,000 × 50%	15,000.00
£180,000	68,126.00

Now think about the situation where Lara makes a personal pension contribution of £16,000 in 2012/13. The contribution will have been paid net of 20% tax. This means that the gross amount of the payment is £16,000 × 100/80 = £20,000 and Lara's basic rate band must be extended by £20,000. Her income tax liability is calculated as follows:

	£
£34,370 × 20%	6,874.00
£20,000 (extended band) × 20%	4,000.00
£115,630 × 40%	46,252.00
£10,000 × 50%	5,000.00
£180,000	62,126.00

The difference between the tax liabilities without and with the Gift Aid donation is £20,000 × (50 – 20)% = £6,000. The total tax relief is:

	£
Basic rate relief given by net payment	4,000.00
Additional rate relief given by extending basic rate band	6,000.00
Total tax relief (50% of contribution)	10,000.00

CALCULATING INCOME TAX PAYABLE

We have seen above how to calculate the income tax liability on non-savings, savings and dividend income. Once this is done there are two final adjustments to be made in order to arrive at the tax payable, which is the balance of the liability still to be settled in cash.

(1) Deduct the tax credit on dividends from the tax liability. Although deductible, this tax credit cannot be repaid if it exceeds the income tax liability.

Task 5

Doris received dividend income of £22,500 in 2012/13. She has no other income.

The tax payable is:

 £

---

(2) Finally deduct any tax deducted at source on savings income, and any tax deducted under the PAYE system by an employer.

These amounts of tax suffered can be repaid to the extent that they exceed the income tax liability.

HOW IT WORKS

Samantha has the following income and outgoings for 2012/13.

	£
Salary (tax deducted by employer £4,000)	25,000
UK dividend received (net)	2,000
Building society interest received (net)	16,400
Qualifying charitable donations paid under Gift Aid (gross amount)	300

Samantha's tax payable for 2012/13 is:

	Non-savings income £	Savings income £	Dividend income £	Total £
Employment income	25,000			
Building Society interest				
£16,400 × 100/80		20,500		
UK dividends				
£2,000 × 100/90			2,222	
Total income	25,000	20,500	2,222	47,722
Less: personal allowance	(8,105)			(8,105)
Taxable income	16,895	20,500	2,222	39,617

	£
Tax on non-savings income	
£16,895 × 20%	3,379.00
Tax on savings income	
£17,475 £(34,370 – 16,895) × 20%	3,495.00
£300 × 20%	60.00
£2,725 × 40%	1,090.00
Tax on dividend income	
£2,222 × 32.5%	722.15
	8,746.15
Less: tax credit on dividend income (£2,222 × 10%)	(222.20)
Less: income tax suffered	
tax on employment income	4,000.00
tax on interest (£20,500 × 20%)	4,100.00
	(8,100.00)
Income tax payable	423.95

Note. The basic rate band is extended by the gross amount of the Gift Aid donation.

Task 6

In 2012/13 Barry has rental income of £31,000, bank interest (net amount received) of £8,000, and UK dividends received of £10,800.

Compute Barry's income tax payable for 2012/13.

Task 7

Kate, who is aged 66, has a salary of £14,955 (tax deducted by employer £900) and building society interest received of £4,000.

Calculate Kate's income tax payable for 2012/13.

CHAPTER OVERVIEW

- We categorise income into different types: non-savings, savings and dividend. Each type of income suffers different rates of tax depending on whether the income falls into the basic, higher or additional rate band

- Non-savings income is taxed first (at 20% then 40% then 50%) then savings income (at 20% then 40% then 50%) and finally dividend income (at 10% then 32.5% then 42.5%)

- The savings income starting rate of 10% applies to savings income within the savings income starting rate band

- Gift Aid donations and personal pension contributions are paid net of basic rate (20%) tax

- Extend the basic rate band by the gross amount of any Gift Aid donations or personal pension contributions paid. This gives further tax relief to higher and additional rate taxpayers

- Deduct the tax credit on dividend income from the income tax liability. However, if it exceeds the income tax liability, the excess cannot be repaid

- Tax suffered on interest and tax deducted under the PAYE system is deducted in computing tax payable and can be repaid

Keywords

Basic rate band – the first £34,370 of income. The basic rate band may be extended by the gross amount of any Gift Aid donations and personal pension contributions paid

Higher rate band – the next £115,630 of income. The upper limit to the higher rate band may be extended by the gross amount of any Gift Aid donations and personal pension contributions paid

Additional rate threshold – is the threshold over which income is taxed at the additional rate

Savings income starting rate band – applies if the taxpayer does not have non-savings income of at least this amount but has savings income

TEST YOUR LEARNING

Test 1

At what rates is income tax charged on non-savings income?

	✓
10%, 20%, 40% and 50%	
40% and 50%	
20% only	
20%, 40% and 50%	

Test 2

In 2012/13, Albert has a salary of £12,000, £2,000 (gross) of building society interest and £3,000 (gross) of UK dividends.

Albert's income tax liability is:

£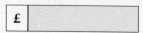

Test 3

In 2012/13 Carol has a salary of £4,000, and has received building society interest of £14,400 and a UK dividend of £19,800.

Carol's income tax liability is:

£

Test 4

In 2012/13 Harry has a salary of £140,000, and has received building society interest of £16,000 and UK dividends of £27,000.

Harry's income tax liability is:

£

Test 5

Explain how tax relief is given on Gift Aid donations.

Test 6

Doreen, who is aged 80, has the following sources of income in 2012/13.

	£
Pension income (tax deducted under PAYE £2,010)	17,000
Property income	3,500
Interest received from NS&I Investment account	380
UK dividends received	630
Premium bond prize	100

Calculate Doreen's income tax payable for the year.

Test 7

Sase has the following income and outgoings in 2012/13.

	£
Business profits	37,000
Building society interest received	4,000
UK dividends received	3,600
Gift Aid donation paid	1,600

Compute Sase's income tax payable for the year.

Test 8

Vince is a higher rate taxpayer and makes a gift aid donation of £15,000 in 2012/13.

What is Vince's basic rate band in 2012/13?

	✓
£49,370	
£34,370	
£46,370	
£53,120	

chapter 6:
SELF-ASSESSMENT
OF INCOME TAX

---

chapter coverage 📖

In this chapter we look at when tax returns must be filed, for how long records must be kept, and at the penalties chargeable for failure to comply with the requirements.

We then look at the due dates for payment of income tax and the consequences of late payment.

Finally, we consider HM Revenue and Customs' powers to check tax returns by raising enquiries.

The topics covered are:

- ✍ Tax returns and keeping records
- ✍ Penalties
- ✍ Payment of tax, interest and penalties for late payment
- ✍ Compliance checks and enquiries

TAX RETURNS AND KEEPING RECORDS

An individual's tax return comprises a Tax Form, together with supplementary pages for particular sources of income and chargeable gains. You may have to complete the supplementary employment or the supplementary land and property pages in your assessment. These forms were included for you to look at earlier in this Text. You will be able to practise completing them in the Personal Tax Question Bank. We will look at chargeable gains and self assessment later in this Text.

Notice of chargeability

Individuals who are chargeable to tax for any tax year and who have not received a notice to file a return are, in general, required to **give notice of chargeability within six months from the end of the tax year**, ie by 5 October 2013 for 2012/13.

Filing tax returns

The FILING DUE DATE is:

- For paper returns – **31 October following the end of the tax year** that the return covers, eg for 2012/13 by 31 October 2013.

- For returns filed online – **31 January following the end of the tax year** that the return covers, eg for 2012/13 by 31 January 2014.

Where a notice to make a return is issued after 31 July following the tax year, a period of three months is allowed for the filing of a paper return.

Where a notice to make a return is issued after 31 October following the tax year, a period of three months is allowed for the online filing of that return.

An individual may ask HMRC to make the tax computation if a paper return is filed. Where an online return is filed, the tax computation is made automatically.

HOW IT WORKS

Advise the following clients of the latest filing date for their personal tax return for 2012/13 if the return is:

(a)   Paper

(b)   Online

Norma   6 April 2013

Melanie   10 August 2013

Olga   12 December 2013

The latest filing dates are:

	Paper	Online
Norma	31 October 2013	31 January 2014
Melanie	9 November 2013	31 January 2014
Olga	11 March 2014	11 March 2014

Task 1

HMRC issued a notice to file a tax return for 2012/13 to Myer on 3 November 2013. She filed this return online on 31 March 2014. State the date by which the return should have been filed:

Keeping of records

Taxpayers must keep and retain all records required to enable them to make and deliver a correct tax return.

In general, records must be retained by tax payers until the later of:

(a)   **One year after the 31 January following the tax year** concerned

(b)   **Five years after 31 January following the tax year** concerned if the taxpayer is in **business or has property business income**

PENALTIES

Penalties for errors in the return

A penalty may be imposed where a taxpayer makes an inaccurate return if he has:

(a) **Been careless** because he has not taken reasonable care in making the return or discovers the error later but does not take reasonable steps to inform HMRC

(b) **Made a deliberate error** but does not make arrangements to conceal it

(c) **Made a deliberate error and has attempted to conceal it**, eg by submitting false evidence in support of an inaccurate figure

An error that is made where the taxpayer has taken reasonable care in making the return and which he does not discover later, does not result in a penalty.

In order for a penalty to be charged, the inaccurate return must result in:

(a) An understatement of the taxpayer's tax liability; or
(b) A false or increased loss for the taxpayer; or
(c) A false or increased repayment of tax to the taxpayer

If a return contains more than one error, a penalty can be charged for each error. The rules also extend to errors in claims for allowances and reliefs and in accounts submitted in relation to tax liability.

The amount of the penalty for error is based on the Potential Lost Revenue (PLR) to HMRC as a result of the error. For example, if there is an understatement of tax, this understatement will be the PLR.

The maximum amount of the penalty for error depends on the type of error.

Type of error	Maximum penalty payable
Mistake	No penalty
Careless	30% of PLR
Deliberate but not concealed	70% of PLR
Deliberate and concealed	100% of PLR

A penalty for error may be reduced if the taxpayer tells HMRC about the error – this is called a disclosure. The reduction depends on the circumstances of the disclosure and the help that the taxpayer gives to HMRC in relation to the disclosure.

An unprompted disclosure is one made at a time when the taxpayer has no reason to believe HMRC has discovered, or is about to discover, the error.

Otherwise, the disclosure will be a **prompted disclosure**. The minimum penalties that can be imposed are as follows.

Type of error	Unprompted disclosure	Prompted disclosure
Careless	0% of PLR	15% of PLR
Deliberate but not concealed	20% of PLR	35% of PLR
Deliberate and concealed	30% of PLR	50% of PLR

You will see that an unprompted disclosure where a careless mistake has been made can reduce a penalty for error to nil, and all penalties can be reduced by half if the taxpayer makes a prompted disclosure.

A penalty for a careless error may be suspended by HMRC to allow the taxpayer to take action to ensure that the error does not occur again (eg where the error has arisen from failure to keep proper records).

HMRC will impose conditions which the taxpayer has to satisfy, eg establishing proper recordkeeping systems.

The penalty will be cancelled if the conditions imposed by HMRC are complied with by the taxpayer within a period of up to two years.

A taxpayer can appeal against:

(a)   The penalty being charged
(b)   The amount of the penalty
(c)   A decision by HMRC not to suspend a penalty
(d)   The conditions set by HMRC in relation to the suspension of a penalty

---

Task 2

Kitty deliberately omitted savings income in her 2012/13 tax return, but did not destroy the evidence of receipt from the building society. She later disclosed this error, before she had reason to believe HMRC might investigate the matter.

Complete the following sentence:

Kitty's penalty can be reduced from ⬚ % of the potential lost revenue (for a deliberate, but not concealed error) to ⬚ %, with the unprompted disclosure of her error.

Penalties for late notification

A penalty can be charged for failure to notify chargeability to income tax and/or capital gains tax that results in a loss of tax. Penalties are behaviour related, increasing for more serious failures, and are based on Potential Lost

Revenue (PLR). This time the PLR is the income tax or capital gains tax which is unpaid on 31 January following the tax year.

The minimum and maximum penalties as percentages of PLR are as follows:

Behaviour	Maximum penalty	Minimum penalty with unprompted disclosure		Minimum penalty with prompted disclosure	
Deliberate and concealed	100%	30%		50%	
Deliberate but not concealed	70%	20%		35%	
		≥12m	<12m	≥12m	<12m
Careless	30%	10%	0%	20%	10%

There is no zero penalty for reasonable care (as there is for penalties for errors on returns – see above), although the penalty may be reduced to 0% if the failure is rectified within 12 months through unprompted disclosure. The penalties may also be reduced at HMRC's discretion in 'special circumstances'. Inability to pay the penalty is not a 'special circumstance'.

The same penalties apply for failure to notify HMRC of a new taxable activity.

Where the taxpayer's failure is not 'deliberate', there is no penalty if he can show he has a 'reasonable excuse'. Reasonable excuse does not include having insufficient money to pay the penalty. Taxpayers can appeal against penalty decisions.

Penalties for late filing

The penalties for filing a late tax return are:

(a) **Immediate £100 penalty** (even if no tax is owing)

(b) **A daily penalty of £10 may be levied** if the return is more than 3 months late (up to maximum 90 days)

(c) **5% of the tax due** if the return is more than 6 months but less than 12 months late

(d) If the return is more than 12 months late the penalty is

- **100% of the tax due** where withholding of information is **deliberate and concealed**

- **70% of the tax due** where withholding of information is **deliberate but not concealed**

- **5% of the tax due in other cases** (eg careless)

These tax based penalties (c) and (d above) are all subject to a minimum of £300.

Penalties for failure to keep records

The maximum penalty for each failure to keep and retain records is **£3,000** per tax year.

PAYMENT OF TAX, INTEREST AND PENALTIES FOR LATE PAYMENT

Payments of tax

A taxpayer must usually make **three payments of income tax:**

Date	Payment
31 January in the tax year	First payment on account
31 July after the tax year	Second payment on account
31 January after the tax year	Final payment to settle any remaining liability

Each PAYMENT ON ACCOUNT is equal to 50% of the income tax payable (after the deduction of tax suffered at source) for the previous year.

Capital gains tax must all be paid on 31 January following the tax year. There are no payments on account of capital gains tax.

HOW IT WORKS

Jeremy paid tax for 2012/13 as follows:

	£
Income tax payable	12,000
Capital gains tax payable	2,000

The payments on account for 2013/14 are:
The income tax payable for 2012/13 was £12,000
Each payment on account is £12,000/2 = £6,000

BPP
LEARNING MEDIA

Task 3

Karen paid tax for 2012/13 as follows:

	£
Income tax payable	14,000
Capital gains tax payable	8,000

Complete the following:

Each payment on account for 2013/14 will be

£ [   ]

They will be due on

[   ]

and

[   ]

Payments on account are not required if the income tax payable for the previous year is less than £1,000, or if more than 80% of the previous year's liability was paid by tax deducted at source.

Payments on account are normally fixed by reference to the previous year's tax liability but if a taxpayer expects his liability to be lower than this, he may claim to reduce his payments on account to:

    (a)   A stated amount

    (b)   Nil

If the taxpayer's eventual liability is higher than he estimated (after making such a claim) he will have reduced the payments on account too far. Although the payments on account will not be adjusted, the taxpayer will suffer an interest charge on late payment.

The balance of any income tax is normally payable on or before the 31 January following the tax year.

HOW IT WORKS

Jameel made payments on account for 2012/13 of £7,500 each on 31 January 2013 and 31 July 2013, based on his 2011/12 liability. He later calculates his total income tax payable for 2012/13 at £20,000. He also calculates that the capital gains tax payable for 2012/13 is £4,900.

The final payment for 2012/13 payable on 31 January 2014 is calculated as follows:

	£
Income tax (£20,000 – £7,500 – £7,500)	5,000
Capital gains tax	4,900
Final payment	9,900

In one case the due date for the final payment is later than 31 January following the end of the year. If a taxpayer has notified chargeability by 5 October but the notice to file a tax return is not issued before 31 October, then the due date for the final payment is three months after the issue of the notice.

Penalties for late payment of tax

Penalties for late payment of tax will be imposed in respect of balancing payments of income tax and any capital gains tax (CGT).

Paid	Penalty
(a) Within 30 days of due date:	none
(b) Not more than six months after the due date:	5% of unpaid tax
(c) More than six months but not more than twelve months after the due date:	a further 5% of unpaid tax
(d) More than twelve months after the due date:	a further 5% of unpaid tax

Penalties for late payment of tax **apply to balancing payments** of income tax and any CGT. They **do not apply to late payments on account**.

Interest

INTEREST is chargeable on **late payment of both payments on account and balancing payments.** In both cases interest runs from the **due date until the day before the actual date of payment.**

If a taxpayer claims to reduce his payments on account and there is still a final payment to be made, interest is normally charged on the payments on account as if each of those payments had been the lower of:

(a)   the reduced amount, plus 50% of the final income tax payable

(b)   the amount which would have been payable had no claim for reduction been made

HOW IT WORKS

Harry made two payments on account of £2,500 each for 2012/13. The payments were made on 31 January 2013 and 31 July 2013. Harry had claimed to reduce these payments from the £4,000 that would have been due had they been based on his previous year's income tax liability.

Harry's 2012/13 tax return showed that his tax liabilities for 2012/13 (before deducting payments on account) were income tax: £10,000; capital gains tax: £3,000. Harry paid the balance of tax due of £8,000 on 30 September 2014.

Harry will be charged interest as follows:

The payments on account should have been £4,000 each. Interest will therefore be charged on the £1,500 not paid on 31 January 2013, from that date until the day before payment (29 September 2014). Similarly, interest will run on the other £1,500 that should have been paid on 31 July 2013 until the day before payment 29 September 2014.

The final balancing payment should have been income tax £2,000 (£10,000 – £8,000) plus capital gains tax £3,000 = £5,000. Interest will run on £5,000 from the due date of 31 January 2014 until the day before payment 29 September 2014.

Note. There would also be a late payment penalty of 10% due on the actual balancing payment of £8,000 (more than 6 months late).

Repayment of tax and repayment interest

Tax is repaid when claimed unless a greater payment of tax is due in the following 30 days, in which case it is set-off against that payment.

Interest is paid on overpayments of:

(a)   Payments on account
(b)   Final payments of income tax and CGT
(c)   Penalties

REPAYMENT INTEREST runs from the **later of the date of overpayment or the date the tax was due until the day before the tax is repaid.** Tax deducted at

source is treated as if it had been paid on the 31 January following the end of the tax year.

COMPLIANCE CHECKS AND ENQUIRIES

HMRC has the power to conduct a compliance check into an individual's tax return.

Some returns are selected for a compliance check at random, others for a particular reason, for example, if HMRC believes that there has been an underpayment of tax due to the taxpayer's failure to comply with tax legislation.

There are two different types of compliance check:

- pre-return checks, which are conducted using its information powers, and

- enquiries into returns, claims or elections which have already been submitted.

Examples of when a pre-return check may be carried out in practice include:

- to assist with clearances or ruling requests

- where a previous check has identified poor record-keeping

- to check that computer systems will produce the information needed to support a return

- to find out about planning or avoidance schemes, and

- where fraud is suspected.

Notice must be given by HMRC of the intention to conduct an enquiry by:

- The first anniversary of the actual filing date; or

- If the return is filed after the due filing date, the quarter day following the first anniversary of the actual filing date. The quarter days are 31 January, 30 April, 31 July and 31 October.

HMRC has only one opportunity to open a formal enquiry and a tax return cannot be subject to a formal enquiry more than once.

In the course of the enquiries the taxpayer may be required to produce documents, accounts or other information. The taxpayer can appeal to the Tax Tribunal against this.

HMRC must issue a closure notice when the enquiries are complete, state the conclusions and amend the self-assessment accordingly. If the taxpayer is not satisfied with the amendment he may, within 30 days, appeal to the Tax Tribunal.

CHAPTER OVERVIEW

- A tax return must be filed by 31 January following a tax year provided it is filed online. Paper returns must be filed by 31 October following the tax year

- A penalty may be imposed if the taxpayer makes an error in his tax return, based on the Potential Loss of Revenue as a result of the error

- A penalty may be imposed if the taxpayer does not notify HMRC of his liability to pay income tax or capital gains tax. The penalty is based on Potential Lost Revenue.

- A fixed penalty of £100 applies if a return is filed late; followed by a potential daily penalty of £10 if the return is filed between three and six months late

- A tax-geared penalty will also apply if a return is filed more than six months late, with a further penalty if this is over twelve months late

- Payments on account of income tax are required on 31 January in the tax year and on 31 July following the tax year

- Balancing payments of income tax and all CGT are due on 31 January following the tax year

- Late payment penalties apply to balancing payments of income tax or any CGT. They do not apply to late payments on account

- Interest is chargeable on late payment of both payments on account and balancing payments

- HMRC can enquire into a return, usually within one year of receipt of the return

Keywords

Filing due date – the date by which a return must be filed

Payment on account – an amount paid on account of income tax

Interest – charged on late payments on account and on late balancing payments

Repayment interest – payable by HMRC on overpaid payments on account, balancing payments and penalties

TEST YOUR LEARNING

Test 1

The due filing date for an income tax return for 2012/13 assuming the taxpayer will submit the return online is:

Test 2

The 2012/13 payments on account will be calculated as

of the income tax payable for

and will be due on

and

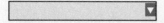

Picklist 1	Picklist 2	Picklist 3	Picklist 4
50%	2012/13	1 January 2014	31 July 2013
25%	2011/12	1 January 2013	31 December 2013
100%	2013/14	31 January 2013	31 January 2014

Test 3

A notice requiring a tax return for 2012/13 is issued in April 2013 and the return is filed online in May 2014. All income tax was paid in May 2014. No payments on account were due.

Explain what charges will be made on the taxpayer?

Test 4

Sase filed her 2012/13 tax return online on 28 January 2014. By what date must HMRC give notice that they are going to enquire into the return? Tick ONE box

	✓
31 January 2015	
31 March 2015	
6 April 2015	
28 January 2015	

Test 5

Jamie paid income tax of £12,000 for 2011/12. In 2012/13, his income tax payable was £16,000.

Jamie's 2012/13 payments on account will each be

£ [   ]

and will be due on

[   ]

and

[   ]

Jamie's balancing payment will be

£ [   ]

and will be due on

[   ]

Test 6

Tim should have made two payments on account of his 2012/13 income tax liability of £5,000 each. He actually made both of these payments on 31 August 2013.

State the amount of any penalties for late payment.

£ [   ]

Test 7

Lola accidentally fails to include an invoice of £17,000 on her 2012/13 tax return. She pays basic rate tax at 20%, and has not yet disclosed this error.

Identify the maximum penalty that could be imposed on her. Tick ONE box

	✓
£5,100	
£3,400	
£1,020	
£2,380	

chapter 7:
COMPUTING CAPITAL GAINS TAX

chapter coverage 📖

In this chapter we see how to compute chargeable gains or allowable losses arising on the disposal of assets, including part disposals of assets.

We see how to set allowable losses against chargeable gains and how to arrive at the net gains taxable in any particular tax year. Then we note how to compute the capital gains tax payable in any particular tax year.

Finally, we look at the special rules that apply when disposals are made to connected people or between married couples/civil partners.

The topics covered are:

- ✍ When does a chargeable gain arise?
- ✍ Computing chargeable gains and allowable losses
- ✍ Part disposals
- ✍ Computing taxable gains in a tax year
- ✍ Computing capital gains tax payable
- ✍ Self assessment for capital gains tax
- ✍ Connected persons
- ✍ Spouses/civil partners
- ✍ Capital gains summary page

WHEN DOES A CHARGEABLE GAIN ARISE?

You saw earlier in this Text that, as a general rule, income is a receipt that is expected to recur (such as rental income), whereas a gain arises on a one-off disposal of a capital asset (eg the sale of an investment property for a profit). For the gain on the disposal of a capital asset to be a chargeable gain there must be a CHARGEABLE DISPOSAL of a CHARGEABLE ASSET by a CHARGEABLE PERSON.

Chargeable persons

Individuals are the only type of chargeable person that you will meet in Personal Tax.

Chargeable disposals

The following are the most important **chargeable disposals:**

- Sales of assets or parts of assets
- Gifts of assets or parts of assets
- The loss or destruction of an asset

A chargeable disposal occurs on the date of the contract (where there is one, whether written or oral), or the date of a conditional contract becoming unconditional.

Exempt disposals include:

- Transfers on death
- Gifts to charities

On death the heirs inherit assets as if they bought them at death for their then market values. There is no capital gain or allowable loss on death.

Chargeable assets

All assets are chargeable assets unless they are specifically designated as exempt.

The following are the exempt assets that you need to be aware of:

- Motor vehicles suitable for private use
- Gilt-edged securities
- Qualifying corporate bonds (QCBs)
- Certain chattels (see later in this Text)
- Premium bonds
- Investments held in an ISA

Any gain arising on disposal of an exempt asset is not taxable and any loss is not allowable.

The exempt asset most commonly appearing in assessment questions is a car. You should not waste time computing a gain or loss on a car. All you need to do is state that the car is an exempt asset, so no gain or loss arises.

Task 1

Which of the following are chargeable assets for CGT purposes?

	Chargeable ✓	Exempt ✓
A diamond necklace		
A cash sum invested in premium bonds that results in a substantial win		
A vintage Rolls Royce		

COMPUTING CHARGEABLE GAINS AND ALLOWABLE LOSSES

Whenever a **chargeable asset** is disposed of, a calculation to determine the amount of any gain or loss is needed. The computation follows a standard format as shown below:

	£
Disposal consideration (or market value)	100,000
Less: incidental costs of disposal	(1,000)
Net proceeds	99,000
Less: allowable costs	(28,000)
Less: enhancement expenditure	(1,000)
Chargeable gain	70,000

We will now look at each of the items in the above pro forma in turn.

Disposal consideration

Usually the disposal consideration is the proceeds of sale of the asset, but a disposal is deemed to take place at market value:

    (a)   Where the disposal is by way of a gift
    (b)   Where the disposal is made for a consideration which cannot be valued
    (c)   Where the disposal is made to a connected person (see below)

Costs

The following costs are deducted in the above pro forma:

(a) **Incidental costs of disposal**

These are the costs of selling an asset. They may include advertising costs, estate agents fees, legal costs or valuation fees. These costs should be deducted separately from any other allowable costs.

(b) **Allowable costs**

These include:

(i) The original purchase price of the asset

(ii) Costs incurred in purchasing the asset (estate agents fees, legal fees etc)

(c) **Enhancement expenditure**

ENHANCEMENT EXPENDITURE is capital expenditure which enhances the value of the asset and is reflected in the state or nature of the asset at the time of disposal.

Task 2

Jack bought a holiday cottage for £25,000. He paid legal costs of £600 on the purchase.

Jack spent £8,000 building an extension to the cottage.

Jack sold the cottage for £60,000. He paid estate agent's fees of £1,200 and legal costs of £750.

Jack's gain on sale is:

£ [   ]

PART DISPOSALS

Sometimes part, rather than the whole of an asset is disposed of. For instance, one-third of a piece of land may be sold. In this case, we need to be able to compute the chargeable gain or allowable loss arising on the part of the asset disposed of.

The problem is that although we know what the disposal proceeds are for the part of the asset disposed of, we do not usually know what proportion of the 'cost' of the whole asset relates to that part. The solution to this is to **use the following fraction to determine the cost of the part disposed of.**

BPP
LEARNING MEDIA

The fraction is:

$$\frac{A}{A+B} = \frac{\text{Value of the part disposed of}}{\text{Value of the part disposed of + Market value of the remainder}}$$

A is the 'gross' proceeds (or market value) before deducting incidental costs of disposal.

You must learn the above formula for use in your assessment.

The formula is used to apportion the cost of the whole asset. If, however, any expenditure was incurred wholly in respect of the part disposed of, it should be treated as an allowable deduction in full for that part and not apportioned. An example of this is incidental selling expenses, which are wholly attributable to the part disposed of.

HOW IT WORKS

Mr Jones bought four acres of land for £270,000. He sold one acre of the land at auction for £200,000, before auction expenses of 15%. The market value of the three remaining acres is £460,000.

The cost of the land being sold is:

$$\frac{200,000}{200,000 + 460,000} \times £270,000 = £81,818$$

	£
Disposal proceeds	200,000
Less: incidental costs of sale (15%)	(30,000)
Net proceeds	170,000
Less: cost (see above)	(81,818)
Chargeable gain	88,182

Task 3

Yarrek bought a plot of land for investment purposes for £100,000. In January 2013, he sold part of the land for £391,000, which was net of legal fees on the sale of £9,000. At that time, the value of the remaining land was £600,000.

The chargeable gain arising on the disposal is:

£ [   ]

COMPUTING TAXABLE GAINS IN A TAX YEAR

An individual pays capital gains tax (CGT) on any **taxable gains** arising in a **tax year** (6 April to 5 April).

Taxable gains are the net chargeable gains (gains minus losses) of the tax year, reduced by unrelieved losses brought forward from previous years and the annual exempt amount.

A standard format is shown below:

	£
Chargeable gains in tax year	100,000
Less: losses in tax year	(27,000)
Net chargeable gains	73,000
Less: capital losses brought forward	(15,000)
Less: annual exempt amount	(10,600)
Taxable gain	47,400

We will look at both of these items in turn.

Annual exempt amount

All individuals are entitled to an annual exempt amount. For 2012/13 it is £10,600. As you can see above, it is the last deduction to be made in computing taxable gains, and effectively means that for 2012/13 the first £10,600 of chargeable gains are tax-free.

Task 4

In 2012/13 Tina has the following gains:

	£
Chargeable gains	18,000

Tina's taxable gains for 2012/13 are:

£ [   ]

Losses

Sometimes an allowable loss rather than a taxable gain arises. Once a loss has been calculated deal with it as follows:

(a) First, set it against gains arising in the same tax year (shown as 'losses in the tax year' in above proforma) until these are reduced to £nil, then

(b) Carry any remaining loss forward to set against net gains in the next tax year but only to reduce the net gains in the next year down to the annual exempt amount. This means the taxpayer does not lose the benefit of the annual exempt amount. Any loss remaining is carried forward.

HOW IT WORKS

(a) Tim has chargeable gains for 2012/13 of £25,000 and allowable losses of £16,000. As the losses are current year losses they must be fully relieved against the gains to produce net gains of £9,000, despite the fact that net gains are below the annual exempt amount.

	£
Chargeable gains in tax year	25,000
Less: losses in tax year	(16,000)
Net chargeable gains	9,000
Less: annual exempt amount	(10,600)
Taxable gain	0

(b) Hattie has gains of £11,000 for 2012/13 and allowable losses brought forward of £6,000. Hattie restricts her loss relief to £400 so as to leave net gains of (£11,000 – £400) = £10,600, which will be exactly covered by the annual exempt amount for 2012/13.

	£
Net chargeable gains	11,000
Less: losses brought forward	(400)
Less: annual exempt amount	(10,600)
Taxable gain	0

The remaining £5,600 of losses will be carried forward to 2013/14.

(c) Mildred has chargeable gains of £2,000 for 2012/13 and losses brought forward from 2011/12 of £12,000. She will leapfrog 2012/13 and carry forward all the brought forward losses to 2013/14. The gains of £2,000 are covered by the annual exempt amount for 2012/13.

Task 5

Sally had chargeable gains of £12,000 and allowable losses of £1,000 in 2012/13. She also had allowable losses of £3,000 brought forward from 2011/12.

The capital losses carried forward to 2013/14 are:

	✓
nil	
£4,000	
£3,000	
£2,600	

COMPUTING CAPITAL GAINS TAX PAYABLE

Taxable gains are chargeable to capital gains tax at the rate of 18% or 28% depending on the individual's taxable income for 2012/13. If the individual is a basic rate taxpayer then CGT is payable at 18% on an amount of taxable gains up to the amount of the taxpayer's unused basic rate band and at 28% on the excess.

HOW IT WORKS

(a) Sally has taxable income (ie the amount after the deduction of the personal allowance) of £10,000 in 2012/13 and made taxable gains (ie gains after deduction of the annual exempt amount) of £20,000 in 2012/13.

Sally's capital gains tax liability is:

£20,000 × 18%   £3,600

The taxable income uses £10,000 of the basic rate
band, leaving £24,370 of the basic rate band unused,
therefore all of the taxable gain is taxed at 18%.

This is payable on 31 January 2014.

(b) Hector has taxable income of £50,000 in 2012/13 and made taxable gains of £10,000 in 2012/13.

Hector's capital gains tax liability is:

£10,000 × 28%   £2,800

All of Hector's basic rate band has been taken up by
the taxable income, therefore the taxable gain is taxed
at 28%.

(c) Isabel has taxable income of £30,000 in 2012/13 and made taxable gains of £25,000 in 2012/13.

Isabel has (£34,370 − £30,000) = £4,370 of her basic rate band unused. Isabel's capital gains tax liability is:

	£
£4,370 × 18%	786.60
£20,630 × 28%	5,776.40
£25,000	6,563.00

Task 6

Sarah made the following chargeable gains and allowable losses in 2012/13.

	£
Gain 17.07.12	21,000
Loss 25.08.12	4,500
Gain 15.11.12	17,500

Sarah pays income tax at the additional rate in 2012/13.

The CGT payable for 2012/13 by Sarah is:

£ [   ]

SELF ASSESSMENT FOR CAPITAL GAINS TAX

A taxpayer who makes chargeable gain(s) in a tax year is usually required to file details of the gain(s) in a tax return. In many cases, the taxpayer will be filing a tax return for income tax purposes and will include the capital gains supplementary pages. You will find copies of these at the end of this chapter.

If, however, the taxpayer only has chargeable gains to report, **he must notify his chargeability to HMRC by 5 October following the end of the tax year.** The penalty for late notification is the same as for late notification of income tax chargeability.

The filing date for the tax return is the same as for income tax and the same penalties apply for CGT as for income tax in relation to late filing and errors on the return.

Capital gains tax is payable on 31 January following the end of the tax year. There are no payments on account. The consequences of late payment of CGT are the same as for late payment of income tax so penalties and interest may be charged. Repayment interest may be paid on overpayments of CGT.

CONNECTED PERSONS

If a disposal is made to a connected person, **the disposal is deemed to take place at the market value of the asset.**

If an **allowable loss arises** on the disposal, it can **only be set against gains** arising in the same or future years from disposals **to the same connected person**, and the loss can only be set off if he or she is still connected with the person making the loss.

BPP
LEARNING MEDIA

For this purpose an individual is connected with:

- His relatives (brothers, sisters, lineal ancestors and lineal descendants)
- The relatives of his spouse/civil partner
- The spouses/civil partners of his and his spouse's/civil partner's relatives

---

Task 7

On 1 August 2012 Holly sold a painting to her sister, Emily for £40,000. The market value of the painting on the date of sale was £50,000. Holly had bought the painting for £60,000.

The allowable loss arising on disposal of the painting by Holly is:

£

Explain how may this be relieved?

SPOUSES/CIVIL PARTNERS

Spouses/civil partners are taxed as two separate people. Each individual has an annual exempt amount, and losses of one individual cannot be set against gains of the other.

Disposals between spouses/civil partners do not give rise to chargeable gains or allowable losses. The disposal is said to be on a 'NO GAIN/NO LOSS' basis. The acquiring spouse/civil partner takes the base cost of the disposing spouse/civil partner.

Task 8

William sold an asset to his wife Kate in May 2012 for £32,000 when its market value was £45,000. William acquired the asset for £14,000 in June 2002.

Calculate the chargeable gain on this transfer. Tick ONE box

	✓
nil	
£18,000	
£31,000	
£13,000	

CAPITAL GAINS SUMMARY PAGE

In your assessment you may be asked to complete the capital gains summary page.

A copy of this page is shown below.

HM Revenue & Customs

Capital gains summary

Tax year 6 April 2012 to 5 April 2013

1 Your name

2 Your unique taxpayer reference (UTR)

Summary of your enclosed computations

You **must** enclose your computations, as well as filling in the boxes – read page CGN 9 of the *notes*.

3 Total gains in the year, before losses

£ · 0 0

4 Total losses of the year – *enter '0' if there are none*

£ · 0 0

5 Losses brought forward and used in the year

£ · 0 0

6 Total gains, after losses but before the annual exempt amount

£ · 0 0

7 Annual exempt amount

£ · 0 0

8 Net chargeable gains (box 6 minus box 7) – *but if box 7 is more than box 6, leave blank*

£ · 0 0

9 Additional liability in respect of non-resident or dual resident trusts

£ · 0 0

10 Losses available to be carried forward to later years

£ · 0 0

11 Losses used against an earlier year's gain (special circumstances apply – *read the notes on page CGN 11*)

£ · 0 0

12 Losses used against income – *amount claimed against 2012–13 income*

£ · 0 0

13 Losses used against income – *amount claimed against 2012–13 income*

£ · 0 0

14 Income losses of 2012–13 set against gains

£ · 0 0

15 Entrepreneurs' relief – *read the notes on pages CGN 7 and CGN 8*

£ · 0 0

Listed shares and securities

16 Number of disposals

17 Disposal proceeds

£ · 0 0

18 Allowable costs (including purchase price)

£ · 0 0

19 Gains in the year, before losses

£ · 0 0

20 If you are making any claim or election, put 'X' in the box

21 If your computations include any estimates or valuations, put 'X' in the box

---

SA108 2009   Tax Return: Capital gains summary: Page CG 1   HMRC 12/08 net

HOW IT WORKS

Lucy Lane has given you the following information about her capital gains position for 2012/13:

Asset sold	Proceeds	Cost
Antique table	£20,000	£11,000
Listed shares	£12,000	£7,500
Unlisted shares	£9,000	£11,700

She also has losses brought forward from 2011/12 of £1,200

This would appear on the return as follows:

Box 1 (name)	Lucy Lane
Box 3	13500.00
Box 4	2700.00
Box 5	200.00
Box 6	10600.00
Box 7	10600.00
Box 8	0.00
Box 10	1000.00 (1,200 – 200 used)
Box 16	1
Box 17	12000.00
Box 18	7500.00
Box 19	4500.00

CHAPTER OVERVIEW

- A chargeable gain arises when there is a chargeable disposal of a chargeable asset by a chargeable person

- Enhancement expenditure can be deducted in computing a chargeable gain if it is reflected in the state and nature of the asset at the time of disposal

- On the part disposal of an asset the formula A/(A + B) must be applied to work out the cost attributable to the part disposed of

- Taxable gains are net chargeable gains for a tax year minus losses brought forward minus the annual exempt amount

- Losses brought forward can only reduce net chargeable gains down to the amount of the annual exempt amount

- The rates of CGT are 18% and 28%, but the lower rate of 18% only applies if and to the extent that the individual has any unused basic rate band

- CGT is payable by 31 January following the end of the tax year

- CGT is self assessed and has the same rules about notification of chargeability, penalties and interest as income tax

- A disposal to a connected person takes place at market value

- For individuals, connected people are broadly brothers, sisters, lineal ancestors and descendants and their spouses/civil partners plus similar relations of a spouse/civil partner

- Losses on disposals to connected people can only be set against gains on disposals to the same connected person

- Disposals between spouses/civil partners take place on a no gain/no loss basis

Keywords

Chargeable person – an individual

Chargeable asset – any asset that is not an exempt asset

Chargeable disposal – a sale or gift of an asset

Exempt disposal – a disposal on which no chargeable gain or allowable loss arises

Enhancement expenditure – capital expenditure that enhances the value of the asset and is reflected in the state or nature of the asset at the time of disposal

Taxable gains – the net chargeable gains of a tax year, after deducting losses brought forward and the annual exempt amount

No gain/no loss disposal – a disposal on which no gain or loss arises

TEST YOUR LEARNING

Test 1

Which of the following constitute chargeable disposals for CGT?

	Chargeable ✓	Exempt ✓
A gift of an antique necklace		
The sale of a building		

Test 2

Yvette buys an investment property for £325,000. She sells the property on 12 December 2012 for £560,000.

Her chargeable gain on sale is:

£ [   ]

Test 3

Richard sells four acres of land (out of a plot of ten acres) for £38,000 in July 2012. Costs of disposal amount to £3,000. The ten-acre plot cost £41,500. The market value of the six acres remaining is £48,000.

The chargeable gain/allowable loss arising is:

	✓
£16,663	
£17,500	
£19,663	
£18,337	

Test 4

Philip has chargeable gains of £171,000 and allowable losses of £5,300 in 2012/13. Losses brought forward at 6 April 2012 amount to £10,000.

The amount is liable to CGT in 2012/13 is:

£ [   ]

The losses carried forward are:

£ [   ]

Test 5

Calculate Martha's CGT liability for 2012/13, assuming she is a higher rate taxpayer and made chargeable gains (before the annual exempt amount) of £23,800 in October 2012.

£ [   ]

Test 6

Decide whether the following statement is True or False.

A loss arising on a disposal to a connected person can be set against any gains arising in the same year or in subsequent years.

	✓
True	
False	

Test 7

Decide whether the following statement is True or False.

No gain or loss arises on a disposal to a spouse/civil partner.

	✓
True	
False	

Test 8

Complete the table by ticking the appropriate box for each scenario.

	Actual proceeds used	Deemed proceeds (market value) used	No gain or loss basis
Paul sells an asset to his civil partner Joe for £3,600			
Grandmother gives an asset to her grandchild worth £1,000			
Sarah sells an asset to best friend Cathy for £12,000 worth £20,000			

chapter 8:
CHATTELS AND PRIVATE RESIDENCES

---

chapter coverage 📖

In this chapter we see how to compute gains and losses arising on the disposal of chattels. We look at the exemption that is available for any gain that arises on the disposal of an individual's private residence.

The topics covered are:

✍ Chattels

✍ Private residences

CHATTELS

A CHATTEL is **tangible moveable property** (ie property that can be moved, seen and touched). Examples are items such as furniture and works of art.

A WASTING CHATTEL is a **chattel with an estimated remaining useful life of 50 years or less.** An example would be a racehorse or a greyhound. **Wasting chattels are exempt from CGT** (so that there are no chargeable gains and no allowable losses). There is one exception to this, being plant and machinery used in the taxpayer's trade, but this is not assessable in your assessment.

Task 1

Jamiel bought a racing greyhound for £6,000. The greyhound was sold for £10,000.

Decide whether the following statement is True or False.

A chargeable gain of £4,000 arises on the disposal.

	✓
True	
False	

There are special rules for calculating gains and losses on non-wasting chattels:

   (a)   If a chattel is not a wasting asset, any gain arising on its disposal will still be exempt from CGT if the asset is sold for gross proceeds of £6,000 or less

   (b)   If sale proceeds exceed £6,000, but the cost is less than £6,000 the gain is limited to:

        $5/3 \times$ (gross proceeds − £6,000)

   (c)   If sale proceeds are less than £6,000, any allowable loss is restricted to that which would arise if it were sold for gross proceeds of £6,000

We will have a look at examples of each of these situations in turn.

HOW IT WORKS

John purchased a painting for £3,000. On 1 January 2013 he sold the painting at auction.

If the gross sale proceeds are £4,000, the gain on sale will be exempt.

If the gross sale proceeds are £8,000 with costs of sale of 10%, the gain arising on the disposal of the painting will be calculated as follows:

	£
Gross proceeds	8,000
Less: incidental costs of sale (10%)	(800)
Net proceeds	7,200
Less: cost	(3,000)
Chargeable gain	4,200
Gain cannot exceed 5/3 × £(8,000 – 6,000)	£3,333

Therefore chargeable gain is £3,333.

Task 2

Jacky purchased a non-wasting chattel for £2,500. On 1 October 2012 she sold the chattel at auction for gross proceeds of £10,000 (which was subject to auctioneer's commission of 5%). The gain arising is:

	✓
nil	
£5,833	
£7,000	
£6,667	

HOW IT WORKS

Magee purchased an antique desk for £8,000. She sold the desk in an auction for £4,750 net of auctioneer's fees of 5% in November 2012.

Magee obviously has a loss and therefore the allowable loss is calculated on **deemed proceeds of £6,000.** The costs of disposal can be deducted from the deemed proceeds of £6,000.

	£
Deemed disposal proceeds	6,000
Less: incidental costs of disposal (£4,750 × 5/95)	(250)
	5,750
Less: cost	(8,000)
Allowable loss	(2,250)

Task 3

Jameel purchased a non-wasting chattel for £8,800 which he sold at auction for £3,600 (which was net of 10% commission).

The allowable loss is:

£ [   ]

Interaction of chattels and part disposals

When the part disposal rules are applied to the sale of 'part of an asset' (seen in Chapter 7), the allocation of the cost between the part disposed of and the remaining asset may then result in the need to consider the chattels rules.

HOW IT WORKS

Miguel owned three vases. He had bought these together for £7,500. He sold one of the vases in October 2012 for £9,000. The other two vases were worth £13,500 at that time. As we know, this is treated as a part disposal of the set.

The gain on sale of one vase

	£
Proceeds	9,000
Less: cost (9,000/(9,000 + 13,500)) x £7,500	(3,000)
Gain	6,000

As the apportioned cost is now < £6,000 the chattel rules will be applied:

Gain cannot exceed 5/3 × £(9,000 – 6,000)	5,000

Note. There are special rules that prevent taxpayers splitting up a set of assets and selling them separately in order to use the £6,000 exemption, but these rules are not in your syllabus.

Task 4

In 2012/13, Mr California sold the following chattels.

Chattel	Cost	Proceeds
	£	£
Vase	800	7,000
Sideboard	7,000	5,000

All proceeds are shown before selling expenses of 5% of the gross proceeds. Compute the chargeable gain or allowable loss on each chattel.

PRIVATE RESIDENCES

A gain arising on the sale of an individual's only or main private residence (PRINCIPAL PRIVATE RESIDENCE) **is exempt from CGT**, providing the taxpayer has occupied (or **is** deemed to have occupied) the residence throughout his period of ownership. Any loss in this case is not allowable.

Spouses/civil partners are entitled to only one principal private residence between them. This applies even though they are generally taxed independently.

The basic rule is that the gain is wholly exempt where the owner has occupied the whole of the residence throughout his period of ownership. Where occupation has been for only part of the period, the proportion of the gain exempted is:

$$\text{Total gain} \times \frac{\text{Period of occupation}}{\text{Total period of ownership}}$$

The last 36 months of ownership is exempt in all cases if, at some time, the residence has been the taxpayer's main residence.

Task 5

Clare bought herself a flat in April 2007 for £80,000. She lived in the flat until March 2010 when she moved to a farmhouse she had bought to be her main residence. The flat was empty until it was sold in March 2013 for £300,000.

Decide whether the following statement is True or False

The gain arising on the sale is completely exempt.

	✓
True	
False	

Deemed occupation

The period of occupation is also deemed to include certain periods of absence, provided the individual had no other main residence at that time and **the period of absence was at some time both preceded by and followed by a period of actual occupation**.

These periods of **deemed occupation** are:

    (a) **Any period** (or periods taken together) of absence, **for any reason**, **not exceeding three years**. Where such a period exceeds three years, three years out of the longer period are deemed to be a period of occupation;

    (b) **Any periods** during which the **owner was required by his employment to live abroad**;

(c) **Any period** (or periods taken together) **not exceeding four years** where the owner was:

    (i) **Self-employed and forced to work away from home** (UK and abroad); or

    (ii) **Employed and required to work elsewhere in the UK** (overseas employment is covered by (b) above).

A period of absence may be treated as deemed occupation under the above rules, even if the residence is let while the owner is away.

Periods of ownership prior to April 1982, whether the property is occupied or not, are ignored.

HOW IT WORKS

Mr A purchased a house for £50,000 on 31 March 1993. He lived in the house until 30 June 1993. He was then sent to work abroad by his employer for five years before returning to the UK to live in the house again on 1 July 1998. He stayed in the house for six months before moving out to live with friends until the house was sold on 31 December 2012 for £150,000.

First work out what periods are chargeable and which are exempt:

		Exempt months	Chargeable months
(i)	1 April 1993 to 30 June 1993	3	–
(ii)	1 July 1993 to 30 June 1998	60	–
(iii)	1 July 1998 to 31 December 1998	6	–
(iv)	1 January 1999 to 31 December 2009	–	132
(v)	1 January 2010 to 31 December 2012	36	–
		105	132

Explanations:

    (i) *April 1993 to June 1993*. Actual occupation.

    (ii) *July 1993 to June 1998*. Covered by the exemption for periods of absence during which the owner is required by his employment to live abroad. The period is both preceded and followed by a period of owner occupation.

    (iii) *July 1998 to December 1998*. Actual occupation.

    (iv) *January 1999 to December 2009*. This period is not eligible to be partly covered by the exemption for three years of absence for any reason, as it is not followed by a period of actual occupation.

    (v) *January 2010 to December 2012*. Covered by the final 36 months exemption.

Then calculate the chargeable gain after the exemption has been applied:

	£
Disposal proceeds	150,000
Less: cost	(50,000)
	100,000
Less: exempt under PPR provisions	
$\dfrac{105}{105+132} \times £100,000$	(44,304)
Chargeable gain	55,696

In this example, had Mr A gone straight to live with friends in July 1998 instead of having six months occupation, he would have lost not only the extra six months, but also the period from July 1993 to June 1998, as this period of absence would lose its status of deemed occupation as the property was not occupied again by the owner prior to sale.

Task 6

Shammima bought a house on 1 May 2006 for £80,000. She lived in the house until 30 April 2007 when she went to stay with her elderly mother for two years. Shammima returned to the house on 1 May 2009 and lived in it until 31 August 2009. She went to live in a new house she had bought on 1 September 2009.

The first house was sold on 28 February 2013 for £200,000. Calculate the gain arising on disposal of the first house.

CHAPTER OVERVIEW

- Wasting chattels are exempt assets for CGT purposes (eg racehorses and greyhounds)

- If a non-wasting chattel is sold for gross proceeds of £6,000 or less any gain arising is exempt. If gross proceeds exceed £6,000 but the cost is less than £6,000 any gain arising on the disposal of the asset is limited to 5/3 × (Gross proceeds − £6,000)

- If the gross proceeds are less than £6,000 on the sale of a non-wasting chattel, any loss otherwise arising is restricted by deeming the gross proceeds to be £6,000

- Any gain arising on the disposal of an individual's principal private residence is exempt from CGT. A loss is not allowable

- Certain periods of non-occupation count as periods of deemed occupation

- The last 36 months of ownership always count as a period of occupation

Keywords

Chattel – tangible moveable property

Wasting chattel – a chattel with an estimated remaining useful life of 50 years or less

Principal private residence – an individual's only or main residence

Deemed occupation – periods during which an individual is treated as having occupied a residence

TEST YOUR LEARNING

Test 1

Mustafa bought a non-wasting chattel for £3,500.

The gain arising if he sells it for:

(a)   £5,800 after deducting selling expenses of £180 is:

£

(b)   £8,200 after deducting selling expenses of £220 is:

£

Test 2

Simon bought a racehorse for £4,500. He sold the racehorse for £9,000 in December 2012.

The gain arising is:

£

Test 3

Santa bought a painting for £7,000. He sold the painting in June 2012 for £5,000.

The loss arising is:

£

Test 4

Provided the property has at some time been the owner's principal private residence, the last .... months of ownership is always an exempt period.

How many months?

	✓
12	
24	
36	
48	

Test 5

Explain three examples of periods of absence from a property which are deemed periods of occupation for the CGT principal private residence exemption.

Test 6

Josephine purchased a house on 1 April 1995 for £60,000 and used it as her main residence until 1 August 1998 when she was sent by her employer to manage the Paris office. She worked and lived in Paris until 31 July 2002. Josephine returned to live in the house on 1 August 2002 but moved out to live in a new house (to be treated as her main residence) on 1 May 2004. The property was sold on 30 November 2012 for £180,000.

Using the proforma below compute the gain on sale.

	£
Proceeds	
Cost	
Gain before PPR exemption	
PPR exemption	
Gain	

Test 7

Noddy is selling his main residence, which he has owned for 25 years. He lived in the house for the first 14 years of ownership, then for the next 5 years he was posted abroad by his employer. He never returned to live in the house during the remainder of his period of ownership.

What fraction of his gain will be exempt under the private residence exemption?

	✓
22/25	
14/25	
17/25	
19/25	

chapter 9:
SHARES

chapter coverage 📖

In this chapter we see how to compute chargeable gains and allowable losses on the disposal of shares.

This is a very important chapter as the computation of gains and losses on the disposal of shares is a key task in your assessment. Shares may be assessed as a long task, so you need to be prepared to set out a computation in the way outlined in this chapter.

The topics covered are:

- ✎ Why special rules are needed for shares
- ✎ Matching rules
- ✎ Share pool
- ✎ Bonus and rights issues
- ✎ Listed and unlisted shares

BPP
LEARNING MEDIA

WHY SPECIAL RULES ARE NEEDED FOR SHARES

Shares present special problems when computing gains or losses on disposal. For instance, suppose that a taxpayer buys some shares in X plc on the following dates:

	No of shares	Cost
		£
5 July 1992	150	195
17 January 1997	100	375
2 July 2012	100	1,000

On 15 June 2012, he sells 220 of his shares for £3,300. **To work out his chargeable gain, we need to be able to identify which shares** out of his three holdings **were actually sold**. Since one share is identical to any other, it is not possible to work this out by reference to factual evidence.

As a result, it has been necessary to devise 'matching rules'. These allow HMRC to identify on a disposal which shares have been sold and so **work out what the allowable cost** (and therefore the gain) **on disposal should be.** These matching rules are considered in detail below.

It is very important that you understand the matching rules. These rules are very regularly assessed and if you do not understand them you will not be able to get any of this part of a task right.

MATCHING RULES

For individuals the matching of the shares sold is in the following order:

(a) **Shares acquired on the same day**

(b) **Shares acquired in the following thirty days** on a FIFO (first in, first out) basis

(c) **Shares from the share pool**. The share pool includes all other shares not acquired on the dates above, and is explained below.

Task 1

Noah acquired shares in Ark Ltd as follows.

2 August 2009	10,000 shares
25 April 2011	10,000 shares
17 June 2012	1,000 shares
19 June 2012	2,000 shares

Noah sold 15,000 shares on 17 June 2012.

Which shares is he selling for capital gains tax purposes?

SHARE POOL

The share pool includes shares acquired up to the day before the disposal on which we are calculating the gain or loss. It grows when an acquisition is made and shrinks when a disposal is made.

The calculation of the share pool value

To compute the value of the share pool, set-up two columns of figures:

(a) The number of shares
(b) The cost of the shares

Each time shares are acquired, both the number and the cost of the acquired shares are added to those already in the pool.

When there is a disposal from the pool, both the number of shares being disposed of, and a cost relating to those shares, are deducted from the pool. The cost of the disposal is calculated as a proportion of total cost in the pool, based on the number of shares being sold.

HOW IT WORKS

Jackie bought 10,000 shares in X plc for £6,000 in August 1993 and another 10,000 shares for £9,000 in December 2005.

She sold 12,000 shares for £24,000 in August 2012.

BPP
LEARNING MEDIA

The share pool is:

	No of shares	Cost
		£
August 1993 Acquisition	10,000	6,000
December 2005 Acquisition	10,000	9,000
	20,000	15,000
August 2012 Disposal	(12,000)	(9,000)
(£15,000 ×12,000/20,000 = £9,000)		
c/f	8,000	6,000

The gain is:

	£
Proceeds of sale	24,000
Less: allowable cost	(9,000)
Chargeable gain	15,000

Task 2

Joraver bought 9,000 shares in Z plc for £4,500 in May 1997. He sold 2,000 shares in August 2006 for £3,500. He then bought a further 5,000 shares for £7,500 in May 2009.

Joraver sold 10,000 shares for £20,000 in January 2013.

The gain on the sale in 2013 is:

£ [   ]

HOW IT WORKS

Tony bought shares in A Ltd as follows.

11 May 2002	14,000 shares for £20,000
9 April 2007	5,000 shares for £12,000
15 June 2012	5,000 shares for £15,000

He sold 18,000 shares for £49,500 on 5 June 2012.

The disposal is matched first against the acquisition in the next 30 days as follows.

	£
Proceeds of sale $\dfrac{5,000}{18,000} \times £49,500$	13,750
Less: allowable cost	(15,000)
Allowable loss	(1,250)

Then the disposal is matched against the share pool.

	£
Proceeds of sale $\dfrac{13,000}{18,000} \times £49,500$	35,750
Less: allowable cost (W)	(21,895)
Chargeable gain	13,855

Therefore the net chargeable gain is:

£(13,855 – 1,250)	12,605

Working	No of shares	Cost
		£
11 May 2002 Acquisition	14,000	20,000
9 April 2007 Acquisition	5,000	12,000
	19,000	32,000
5 June 2012 Disposal	(13,000)	(21,895)
c/f	6,000	10,105

Task 3

Eliot acquired shares in K Ltd as follows.

10 August 2004	5,000 shares for £10,000
15 April 2007	2,000 shares for £5,000
25 July 2012	1,000 shares for £3,800
27 July 2012	500 shares for £1,700

Eliot sold 6,000 shares for £21,600 on 25 July 2012.

Calculate the net chargeable gain arising on the disposal by Eliot.

BONUS AND RIGHTS ISSUES

Bonus issues

BONUS SHARES are **additional shares given free to shareholders based on their current holding(s).** For example, a shareholder may own 2,000 shares. The company makes a 1 share for every 2 shares held bonus issue (called 1 for 2 bonus issue). The shareholder will then have an extra 1,000 shares, giving him 3,000 shares overall.

Bonus shares are treated as being acquired at the date of the original acquisition of the underlying shares giving rise to the bonus issue.

Since bonus shares are issued at no cost there is **no need to adjust the original cost.**

Rights issues

In a RIGHTS ISSUE, a **shareholder is offered the right to buy additional shares by the company in proportion to the shares he already holds.**

The difference between a bonus issue and a rights issue is that in a rights issue the new shares are paid for. This results in an **adjustment to the original cost.**

HOW IT WORKS

Jonah acquired 20,000 shares for £36,000 in T plc in April 2002. There was a 1 for 2 bonus issue in May 2007 and a 1 for 5 rights issue in August 2012 at £1.20 per share.

Jonah sold 30,000 shares for £45,000 in December 2012.

The share pool is constructed as follows:

	No of shares	Cost £
April 2002 Acquisition	20,000	36,000
May 2007 Bonus 1 for 2	10,000	–
	30,000	36,000
August 2012 Rights 1 for 5 @ £1.20	6,000	7,200
	36,000	43,200
December 2012 Disposal	(30,000)	(36,000)
c/f	6,000	7,200

The gain on sale is:

	£
Proceeds of sale	45,000
Less: allowable cost	(36,000)
Chargeable gain	9,000

Task 4

Dorothy bought 2,000 shares for £10,000 in S Ltd in August 2002. There was a 1 for 1 rights issue at £2.50 in May 2005 and Dorothy took up all her rights issue shares. There was a 1 for 4 bonus issue in September 2008.

Dorothy sold 3,000 shares for £18,000 in October 2012.

Her chargeable gain on sale is:

£ [   ]

LISTED AND UNLISTED SHARES

The capital gains summary pages require you to show gains on listed and unlisted shares separately. There is no difference in the computation of gains.

LISTED SHARES are listed on a Stock Exchange. A listed company will always have the letters plc (public limited company) in its name.

UNLISTED SHARES are not listed on a Stock Exchange. An unlisted company will have either Ltd (Limited) or plc (public limited company) in its name.

You should be told in the assessment whether shares are listed or unlisted if relevant.

CHAPTER OVERVIEW

- The matching rules for individuals are:

  - Same day acquisitions
  - Next 30 days acquisitions on a FIFO basis
  - Shares in the share pool

- The share pool runs up to the day before disposal

- Bonus issue and rights issue shares are acquired in proportion to the shareholder's existing holding

- The difference between a bonus and a rights issue is that in a rights issue shares are paid for

- Listed shares are listed on a Stock Exchange, unlisted shares are not listed on a Stock Exchange

Keywords

Bonus shares – shares that are issued free to shareholders based on original holdings

Rights issues – similar to bonus issues except that in a rights issue shares must be paid for

Listed shares – shares listed on a Stock Exchange

Unlisted shares – shares not listed on a Stock Exchange

TEST YOUR LEARNING

Test 1

Tasha bought 10,000 shares in V plc in August 1992 for £5,000 and a further 10,000 shares for £16,000 in April 2007. She sold 15,000 shares for £30,000 in November 2012.

Her chargeable gain is:

	✓
£9,000	
£11,500	
£17,000	
£14,250	

Test 2

Decide whether the following statement is True or False.

In both a bonus issue and a rights issue, there is an adjustment to the original cost of the shares.

	✓
True	
False	

Test 3

Marcus bought 2,000 shares in X plc in May 2001 for £12,000. There was a 1 for 2 rights issue at £7.50 per share in December 2002. Marcus sold 2,500 shares for £20,000 in March 2013.

His chargeable gain is:

£

Test 4

Mildred bought 6,000 shares in George plc in June 2009 for £15,000. There was a 1 for 3 bonus issue in August 2010. Mildred sold 8,000 shares for £22,000 in December 2012.

Her chargeable gain is:

£

ANSWERS TO CHAPTER TASKS

CHAPTER 1   The tax framework

1

31 January 2019

2   The following have the force of law:

	✓
Acts of Parliament	✓
HMRC Statements of practice	
Statutory Instruments	✓
Extra statutory concessions	

3   You should tell Cornelius that under the AAT *Guidelines* on client confidentiality, you cannot provide him with any information on another client without the specific authority of that client.

CHAPTER 2   Employment income

1

Factor	contract of service	contract for services
Leon must accept further work if offered	✓	
Leon hires his own helpers		✓
Leon is entitled to paid holidays	✓	
Leon can profit from sound management		✓

2   Rio's earnings for 2012/13 are:

£	20,625

£20,000 × 9/12 plus £22,500 × 3/12.

The bonus is received when Rio becomes entitled to it, which is in the following tax year (2013/14). It is not linked to the period during which it was earned (the company's period of account).

3   Rita receives the bonus on:

	✓
31 December 2012	
31 March 2013	
10 April 2013	✓
15 June 2013	
31 July 2013	
31 October 2014	

This is the date when the amount is determined (after the date the company's period of account ends).

4   The taxable benefit on the provision of the car in 2012/13 is:

£	2,400

The CO_2 emissions of the car are 205g/km (rounded down to the nearest five below)

Amount over baseline figure 205 – 100 = 105g/km

Divide by 5 = 21

The taxable percentage is 11% + 21% = 32%

So the benefit is 32% × £10,000 × 9/12 = £2,400

Note. The benefit is multiplied by 9/12 as the car was only available for nine months in the tax year.

5   The total taxable benefit arising to Nissar in 2012/13 is:

£	15,060

Round down CO_2 emissions to 180 g/km

Amount above baseline: 180 – 100 = 80 g/km

Divide by 5 = 16

Taxable % = 11% + 16% + 3% (diesel) = 30%

	£
Car benefit £30,000 × 30%	9,000
Fuel benefit £20,200 × 30%	6,060
Total benefit	15,060

Note. No deduction is made in respect of the amount paid towards the cost of private fuel.

6   The taxable benefit for use arising in 2011/12 is:

£ | 1,200

Use benefit £6,000 × 20%

and in 2012/13 is:

£ | 300

Use benefit £6,000 × 20% × 3/12

and the taxable benefit on Ahmed's acquisition in 2012/13 is:

£ | 3,500

Acquisition	£	£
(i) Market value at acquisition	4,000	–
(ii) Market value when first provided	–	6,000
Less: assessed in respect of use		
£(1,200 + 300)	–	(1,500)
	4,000	4,500
Less: amount paid	(1,000)	(1,000)
	3,000	3,500

Take higher, £3,500

7   The taxable benefit arising in respect of the loan in 2012/13 assuming no elections are made is:

£ | 228

$$\frac{£6,200 + £5,200}{2} \times 4\%$$

As no elections are made, the 'average' method of valuing the loan is used.

8   The total taxable benefit is:

£ | 1,400

Interest: no benefit because loan not over £5,000.

Loan written-off: £4,000 × 35% = taxable benefit.

9 The taxable value of the accommodation provided in 2012/13 is:

	✓
£9,000	
£14,200	✓
£26,200	
£21,000	

	£
Annual value	5,200
Additional benefit £(600,000 – 75,000) × 4%	21,000
	26,200
Less: rent paid	(12,000)
Taxable benefit	14,200

10 Mr Quinton's taxable employment income for 2012/13 is:

£	29,540

	£	£
Salary (= net earnings)		27,400
Accommodation benefits		
Annual value: exempt (job-related)		
Ancillary services		
Electricity	550	
Gas	400	
Gardener	750	
Redecoration	1,800	
	3,500	
Restricted to 10% of £27,400	2,740	
Less: employee's contribution (12 × £50)	(600)	
		2,140
Employment income		29,540

11

£	40

	£	£
Amount received 12,000 × 42p		5,040
Less: statutory limit		
10,000 × 45p	4,500	
2,000 × 25p	500	
		(5,000)
Taxable benefit		40

12

£	2,000

	£
Amount received 12,000 × 25p	3,000
Less: statutory limit	
(10,000 × 45p)	
(2,000 × 25p)	
	(5,000)
Allowable deduction	(2,000)

CHAPTER 3   Property income

1   Harry's taxable rental income for 2012/13 is:

£	1,000

	£
Rental income (net of bad debt)	1,300
Rental income (£400 × 1)	400
Less: interest	(700)
Taxable property income	1,000

2   Johnson's taxable property income for 2012/13 is:

£	10,475

	£	£
Rental income: property 1 (accrued)		14,000
property 2 (3/12 × £6,800)		1,700
Less: agent's fees		
(15% × £(14,000 + 1,700))	2,355	
insurance on Whitehouse		
(3/12 × £1,200) + (9/12 × £1,400)	1,350	
insurance on Blackhouse		
(3/12 × £980) + (9/12 × £1,100)	1,070	
advertising for tenants	450	
		(5,225)
Taxable property income		10,475

3 Sunita's taxable property income for 2012/13 is:

	✓
£8,070	✓
£7,900	
£9,100	
£9,270	

	£	£
Rental income		12,000
Less: water rates	800	
council tax	900	
agents fees (10% x £12,000)	1,200	
wear and tear allowance		
10% × £(12,000 – 800 – 900)	1,030	
		(3,930)
Taxable property income		8,070

4 Neither property qualifies.

Property 1 is not available for let for the qualifying 210 days, and property 2 is not actually let for the qualifying 105 days.

It is possible to aggregate the periods of actual letting to give an average period, however this would still be less than the 105 days on average. (110 days plus 95 days gives an average of 102.5 days).

5 Jordan and Merry each receive rental income of £(80 × 52)/2 = £2,080. They each have a rent-a-room limit of £2,125. Since the rental is less than the limit, the rent is wholly exempt from income tax for them. The expenses are ignored. It is possible to elect to ignore rent-a-room relief but this will not be beneficial in this case.

CHAPTER 4 Taxable income

1 The total amount of interest on which Jesse will be taxable is:

£	260

Building society £160 × 100/80 = £200

Plus NS&I investment account = £60

2 The gross amounts of dividends to be included in her income tax computation are:

£	1,000

(£900 × 100/90)

and the gross amounts of interest to be included in her income tax computation are:

£	2,000

(£1,600 × 100/80)

3 The total amount taxable on Denis is:

	✓
£280	
£500	
£100	✓
£680	

NatWest deposit a/c interest

£80 × 100/80 = £100

Dividend income on an ISA and interest on the maturity of NS&I savings certificates are exempt from income tax.

4

	Non-savings income £	Savings income £	Dividend income £	Total £
Business income	44,000			
Building society interest		2,000		
Dividends			1,000	
Total income	44,000	2,000	1,000	47,000

Lotto winnings are exempt from income tax.

5

	Non-savings income £	Savings income £	Dividend income £	Total £
Trade profits	10,000			
Building society interest (× 100/80)		2,500		
Dividends (× 100/90)			5,000	
Total income	10,000	2,500	5,000	17,500
Less: personal allowance	(8,105)			(8,105)
Taxable income	1,895	2,500	5,000	9,395

Premium bond prizes are exempt from income tax.

6 The personal allowance that Zelda is entitled to in 2012/13 is:

£	5,605

	Non-savings income £	Savings income £	Dividend income £	Total £
Employment income	97,500			
Bank interest (× 100/80)		5,000		
Dividends (× 100/90)			2,500	
Total income	97,500	5,000	2,500	105,000

	£
Total income	105,000
Less: income limit	(100,000)
Excess	5,000
Personal allowance	8,105
Less: half excess	(2,500)
Amount available	5,605

7   Ernest is entitled to a personal allowance in 2012/13 of:

£	3,855

	£
Total income	109,000
Less: Gift Aid donation	(500)
Adjusted total income	108,500
Less: income limit	(100,000)
Excess	8,500
Personal allowance	8,105
Less: half excess	(4,250)
Adjusted personal allowance	3,855

8   The age allowance that Zebedee is entitled to in 2012/13 is:

£	9,360

	Non-savings Income £	Savings income £	Dividend income £	Total £
Pension income	20,500			
Bank interest (× 100/80)		2,500		
Dividends (× 100/90)			5,000	
Total income	20,500	2,500	5,000	28,000

	£
Total income	28,000
Less: income limit	(25,400)
Excess	2,600
Age allowance	10,660
Less: half excess	(1,300)
Adjusted age allowance	9,360

9   The age allowance that Zaza is entitled to in 2012/13 is:

£	8,105

	£
Total income	33,500
Less: income limit	(25,400)
Excess	8,100
Age allowance	10,500
Less: half excess	(4,050)
Minimum age allowance	8,105

CHAPTER 5   Calculation of income tax

1   Her income tax liability is:

> £ | 17,126.00

	Non-savings income £	Savings income £	Total £
Taxable income	25,000	35,000	60,000
Tax on non-savings income			
£25,000 × 20%			5,000.00
Tax on savings income			
(£34,370 – £25,000) = £9,370 × 20%			1,874.00
£25,630 × 40%			10,252.00
£60,000			
Tax liability			17,126.00

2   Stacey's income tax liability is:

> £ | 61,501.00

	£
Non-savings income	
£34,370 × 20%	6,874.00
£85,630 × 40%	34,252.00
£120,000	
Dividend income	
£30,000 × 32.5%	9,750.00
£25,000 × 42.5%	10,625.00
£175,000	
Income tax liability	61,501.00

3 Joe's income tax liability for 2012/13 is:

£	997.50

	Non-savings income £	Savings income £	Total £
Employment income	9,000		
Bank interest (£4,000 × 100/80)		5,000	
Total income	9,000	5,000	14,000
Less: personal allowance	(8,105)		(8,105)
Taxable income	895	5,000	5,895

Tax on non-savings income	
£895 × 20%	179.00
Tax on savings income	
£(2,710 – 895) = 1,815 × 10%	181.50
£(5,000 – 1,815) = 3,185 × 20%	637.00
Income tax liability	997.50

4 Hans' tax liability for 2012/13 is:

£	11,726.00

	Non-savings income £	Savings income £	Total £
Taxable income	24,000	26,000	50,000

Tax on non-savings income	
£24,000 × 20%	4,800.00
Tax on savings income	
£10,370 (£34,370 – £24,000) × 20%	2,074.00
£7,000 (£5,600 × 100/80) × 20%	1,400.00
£8,630 × 40%	3,452.00
£50,000	11,726.00

Note. The basic rate band is extended by the gross amount of the personal pension contribution paid.

5   The tax payable is:

£	0

	Dividend income
	£
Dividends (× 100/90)	25,000
Less: personal allowance	(8,105)
Taxable income	16,895

	£
Tax on dividend income	
£16,895 × 10%	1,689.50
Less: tax credit on dividend (max)	(1,689.50)
Tax payable	nil

6

	Non-savings income	*Savings income*	*Dividend income*	*Total*
	£	£	£	£
Rental income	31,000			
Bank interest (× 100/80)		10,000		
Dividends (× 100/90)			12,000	
Total income	31,000	10,000	12,000	53,000
Less: personal allowance	(8,105)			(8,105)
Taxable income	22,895	10,000	12,000	44,895
Tax on non-savings income				
£22,895 × 20%				4,579.00
Tax on savings income				
£10,000 × 20%				2,000.00
Tax on dividend income				
£1,475 £(34,370 – 22,895 – 10,000) × 10%				147.50
£10,525 × 32.5%				3,420.62
44,895				
Income tax liability				10,147.12
Less: tax credit on dividend				(1,200.00)
tax suffered on interest				(2,000.00)
Income tax payable				6,947.12

7

	Non-savings Income £	Savings income £	Total £
Employment income	14,955		
Building society interest (× 100/80)		5,000	
Total income	14,955	5,000	19,955
Less: personal allowance	(10,500)		(10,500)
Taxable income	4,455	5,000	9,455

	£
Tax on non-savings income	
£4,455 × 20%	891.00
Tax on savings income	
£5,000 × 20%	1,000.00
Tax liability	1,891.00
Less: tax deducted from employment income	(900.00)
tax suffered on building society interest	(1,000.00)
Tax repayable	(9.00)

Note that both tax suffered on building society interest and tax suffered on employment income are deducted from the tax liability to arrive at tax payable. As these amounts have exceeded the tax liability, the excess can be repaid.

CHAPTER 6   Self-assessment of income tax

1   2 February 2014

Since the notice to file was issued after 31 October 2013, the filing date is three months after the notice was issued.

2   Kitty's penalty can be reduced from 70 % of the potential lost revenue (for a deliberate, but not concealed error) to 20 %, with the unprompted disclosure of her error.

3 Each payment on account for 2013/14 will be

£ | 7,000

Payments on account $\dfrac{£14,000}{2}$

No payments on account are due in respect of CGT.

They will be due on

31 January 2014

and

31 July 2014

CHAPTER 7 Computing capital gains tax

1

	Chargeable ✓	Exempt ✓
A diamond necklace	✓	
A cash sum invested in premium bonds that results in a substantial win		✓
A vintage Rolls Royce		✓

2 Jack's gain on sale is:

£ | 24,450

	£
Proceeds of sale	60,000
Less: costs of disposal £(1,200 + 750)	(1,950)
Net proceeds of sale	58,050
Less: original cost	(25,000)
costs of acquisition	(600)
enhancement expenditure	(8,000)
Chargeable gain	24,450

3   The chargeable gain arising on the disposal is:

£ | 351,000

	£
Proceeds	400,000
Less: costs of disposal	(9,000)
Net proceeds of sale	391,000
Less: cost	
(400,000/400,000 + 600,000) × £100,000	(40,000)
Chargeable gain	351,000

4   Tina's taxable gains for 2012/13 are:

£ | 7,400

(18,000 – £10,600)

5   The capital losses carried forward to 2013/14 are:

	✓
nil	
£4,000	
£3,000	
£2,600	✓

	£
Chargeable gains	12,000
Less: allowable losses	(1,000)
	11,000
Less: capital losses b/f	(400)
Net gain	10,600
Losses c/f £2,600 £(3,000 – 400)	

6 The CGT payable for 2012/13 by Sarah is:

£	6,552.00

	£
Chargeable gains	38,500
Less: loss	(4,500)
	34,000
Less: Annual exempt amount	(10,600)
Taxable gains	23,400
CGT payable	
£23,400 × 28%	6,552.00

7 The allowable loss arising on disposal of the painting by Holly is:

£	(10,000)

	£
Deemed proceeds (market value)	50,000
Less: cost	(60,000)
Allowable loss	(10,000)

The loss may only be set against gains arising on the disposal of other assets by Holly to Emily.

8

	✓
nil	✓
£18,000	
£31,000	
£13,000	

William transfers the asset to his wife Kate on a 'no gain/no loss' basis. This assumes that William sold it for 'deemed proceeds' equal to his original cost ie £14,000. The market value and the actual proceeds received are not relevant.

CHAPTER 8 Chattels and private residences

1

	✓
True	
False	✓

No chargeable gain/allowable loss arises as greyhounds are exempt assets as they are wasting chattels.

2 The gain arising is:

	✓
nil	
£5,833	
£7,000	
£6,667	✓

	£
Gross proceeds	10,000
Less: commission (5%)	(500)
	9,500
Less: cost	(2,500)
	7,000

Maximum gain 5/3 × £(10,000 – 6,000) = £6,667

3 The allowable loss is:

£	(3,200)

	£
Deemed proceeds	6,000
Less: commission (£3,600 × 10/90)	(400)
	5,600
Less: cost	(8,800)
Allowable loss	(3,200)

4 (a)

The vase	£
Proceeds	7,000
Less: selling expenses (£7,000 × 5%)	(350)
	6,650
Less: cost	(800)
Chargeable gain	5,850

The gain is the lower of £5,850 and £(7,000 – 6,000) × 5/3 = £1,667, so it is $\underline{£1,667}$.

(b)

The sideboard	£
Proceeds (deemed)	6,000
Less: selling expenses (5,000 × 5%)	(250)
	5,750
Less: cost	(7,000)
Allowable loss	(1,250)

5

	✓
True	✓
False	

Clare was in actual occupation from April 2007 to March 2010.

The last 36 months of ownership are exempt because Clare had previously lived in the flat as her only or main residence.

6

First House	Actual or deemed occupation months	Non-occupation months
1 May 2006 to 30 April 2007	12	
1 May 2007 to 30 April 2009	24	
(2 years any reason)		
1 May 2009 to 31 August 2009	4	
1 September 2009 to 28 February 2010		6
1 March 2010 to 28 February 2013	36	
	76	6

	£
Sale proceeds	200,000
Less: cost	(80,000)
	120,000
Less: £120,000 × 76/82	(111,220)
Chargeable gain	8,780

CHAPTER 9   Shares

1   Noah will match his disposal with the 1,000 shares bought on the same day as the disposal, then the 2,000 shares he buys within the next 30 days, and then 12,000 shares from the 20,000 shares which are in the pool.

2   The gain on the sale in 2013 is:

£	10,833

Share pool

	No of shares	Cost
		£
May 1997 Acquisition	9,000	4,500
August 2006 Disposal	(2,000)	(1,000)
c/f	7,000	3,500
May 2009 Acquisition	5,000	7,500
	12,000	11,000
January 2013 Disposal	(10,000)	(9,167)
c/f	2,000	1,833

Gain:

	£
Proceeds of sale	20,000
Less: cost	(9,167)
Chargeable gain	10,833

3   Match the disposal first with the same day acquisition:

	£
Proceeds of sale $\dfrac{1,000}{6,000} \times £21,600$	3,600
Less: cost	(3,800)
Allowable loss	(200)

Then match with the acquisition in the next 30 days:

	£
Proceeds of sale $\dfrac{500}{6,000} \times £21,600$	1,800
Less: allowable cost	(1,700)
Chargeable gain	100

Finally, match with the share pool:

	£
Proceeds of sale $\dfrac{4,500}{6,000} \times £21,600$	16,200
Less: allowable cost (W)	(9,643)
Chargeable gain	6,557

The net chargeable gain is therefore:
£(100 + 6,557 − 200) = £6,457

Working

	No. of shares	Cost £
10 August 2004 Acquisition	5,000	10,000
15 April 2007 Acquisition	2,000	5,000
	7,000	15,000
25.7.12 Disposal	(4,500)	(9,643)
c/f	2,500	5,357

4 Her chargeable gain on sale is:

£	9,000

	£
Proceeds of sale	18,000
Less: allowable cost (W)	(9,000)
Chargeable gain	9,000

Working

Share pool	No. of shares	Cost £
August 2002 Acquisition	2,000	10,000
May 2005 Rights issue 1 for 1 @ £2.50	2,000	5,000
c/f	4,000	15,000
September 2008 Bonus 1 for 4	1,000	–
	5,000	15,000
October 2012 Disposal	(3,000)	(9,000)
c/f	2,000	6,000

CHAPTER 1   The tax framework

1

	✓
True	
False	✓

Most taxpayers have all their tax deducted at source and are not sent a tax return.

2   The two sources of tax law are:

statute law

and

case law

3

	✓
When in a social environment	
When discussing client affairs with third parties with the client's proper and specific authority	✓
When reading documents relating to a client's affairs in public places	
When preparing tax returns	

BPP
LEARNING MEDIA

4

	✓
HMRC	
Nearest police station	
Serious Organised Crime Agency	✓
Tax Tribunal	

5

	✓
The Chancellor of the Exchequer	
Companies House	
HM Revenue and Customs	✓
Members of Parliament	

CHAPTER 2   Employment income

1 Someone is regarded as self-employed if he has a contract for services ,
whereas if he has a contract of service , he will be regarded as an
employee.

2 Expenses are deductible in computing taxable earnings if they are
incurred wholly , exclusively , and necessarily in the
performance of the duties of employment.

3 The amounts that are taxable/(deductible) in calculating employment
income are:

£ (800)

	£
Amount received 8,000 × 35p	2,800
Less: Statutory limit 8,000 × 45p	(3,600)
Deductible amount	(800)

4 The taxable value of this benefit for 2012/13 is:

£ 5,900

being the higher of the annual value and rent actually paid by the employer

5

	✓
True	
False	✓

There is a taxable fuel benefit unless the employer is fully reimbursed for private fuel.

6

	✓
£325	
£400	
£175	
£250	✓

Benefit is based on the higher of:

		£	£
(a)	Current MV		325
(b)	Original MV	500	
	Less: already assessed (in 2011/12)		
	£500 × 20%	(100)	
		400	

ie £400

Therefore the taxable benefit after deduction of the amount paid (£150) is £250.

7

	✓
True	
False	✓

Only if total loans do not exceed £5,000 at any time in the tax year is it ignored.

8   The taxable benefit arising in respect of the car is:

£ | 6,000

CO$_2$ emissions = 170 g/km (rounded down)

Above baseline 170 – 100		=	70 g/km
Divide by 5	= 70/5	=	14
Percentage	= 11% + 14%	=	25%
Benefit 25% × £24,000		=	£6,000

9   The total taxable benefits are:

£ | 25,816

	£
Car benefit (W)	20,160
Fuel benefit (£20,200 × 28%)	5,656
Telephone benefit (exempt – one mobile phone)	NIL
Total benefit	25,816

Working

Amount of emissions above baseline 185 – 100 = 85 g/km
Divide by 5 = 17
Percentage = 11% + 17% = 28%
£72,000 × 28% = £20,160

10

Item	Taxable	Exempt
Write off loan of £2,000 (only loan provided)	✓	☐
Payments by employer of £500 per month into registered pension scheme	☐	✓
Provision of mobile phone	☐	✓
Provision of a company car for both business and private use	✓	☐
Removal costs of £5,000	☐	✓
Accommodation provided to enable the employee to spend longer time in the office	✓	☐

CHAPTER 3   Property income

1   The rental income taxable in 2012/13 is:

£ | 1,200

Rent accrued 1 December 2012 to 5 April 2013 = 4/12 × £3,600

2   Relief for wear and tear of furnishings is:

	✓
£1,600	
£1,490	✓
£1,568	
£1,522	

10% × £(16,000 – 320 – 780)

3   How much would be allowed against his rental income for 2012/13?

£ | 5,000

Insurance premiums accrued in 2012/13:

	£
6/12 × £4,800	2,400
6/12 × £5,200	2,600
	5,000

4   Losses from furnished holiday lettings can only be carried forward against future profits from the same furnished holiday lettings business.

5   The income qualifies as earnings for pension purposes. Primarily this gives scope for relief for pension contributions.

6   What is his taxable rental income for 2012/13?

£ | 1,667

	£
Rental income (£4,000 × 9/12)	3,000
Less: bad debt (£4,000 × 1/12)	(333)
expenses	(1,000)
Taxable rental income	1,667

Rent of £5,000 paid 4 April 2013 accrues in 2013/14 and is therefore taxed in that year.

7 What is the maximum rental income in a tax year which is exempt from income tax under the rent-a-room scheme?

	✓
£2,125	
£4,250	✓
£4,500	
£8,105	

8 Which TWO of the following are not advantages of a property being classed as a furnished holiday let?

	✓
Income can qualify as 'earnings' for pension purposes	
Capital allowances can be claimed on furniture	
Wear and tear allowance can be claimed on furniture	✓
Losses can be set against other income not just property income	✓

CHAPTER 4   Taxable income

1

	Non-savings income	Savings income	Dividend income
Employment income	✓	☐	☐
Dividend received	☐	☐	✓
Property income	✓	☐	☐
Bank interest	☐	✓	☐
Pension income	✓	☐	☐
Interest on government stock	☐	✓	☐

2

	£
Building society interest received of £240 (× 100/80)	300
Interest received on an individual savings account of £40	0
Dividends received of £144 (× 100/90)	160
Interest from government gilts of £350 (received gross)	350

3

	Non-savings income £	Dividend income £	Total £
Employment income	30,000		
Dividends (× 100/90)		300	
Total income	30,000	300	30,300
Less: personal allowance	(8,105)		(8,105)
Taxable income	21,895	300	22,195

Interest on National Savings Certificates is exempt from income tax.

4

	Non-savings income £	Savings income £	Total £
Property income	3,000		
Building society interest			
(7,200 × 100/80)		9,000	
Total income	3,000	9,000	12,000
Less: personal allowance	(3,000)	(5,105)	(8,105)
Taxable income	NIL	3,895	3,895

The personal allowance is deducted first from non-savings income and then from savings income.

5

	Non-savings income £	Savings income £	Dividend income £	Total £
Employment income	110,000			
Interest (× 100/80)		5,000		
Dividends (× 100/90)			4,000	
Total income	110,000	5,000	4,000	119,000
Less: personal allowance (w)	(Nil)			(Nil)
Taxable income	110,000	5,000	4,000	119,000

	£
Total income	119,000
Less: income limit	(100,000)
Excess	19,000
Personal allowance	8,105
Less: half excess	(9,500)
Adjusted personal allowance	Nil

The prize is exempt from income tax.

6 The age allowance available to Zoreen for 2012/13 is:

£ | 8,105

	Non-savings income £	Savings income £	Dividend income £	Total £
Pension income	20,380			
Bank interest (× 100/80)		5,000		
Dividends (× 100/90)			6,000	
Total income	20,380	5,000	6,000	31,380

	£
Total income	31,380
Less: income limit	(25,400)
Excess	5,980

	£
Age allowance	10,660
Less: half excess	(2,990)
	7,670
But cannot be less than	8,105

7   The age allowance available to Escamillo for 2012/13 is:

£ | 9,950

	£
Total income	27,500
Less: Gift aid donation	(1,000)
Adjusted total income	26,500
Less: income limit	(25,400)
Excess	1,100

	£
Age allowance	10,500
Less: half excess	(550)
Adjusted age allowance	9,950

8

	✓
True	
False	✓

The tax credit attached to a dividend can be offset against a taxpayer's tax liability, but if it exceeds the liability the taxpayer cannot receive a repayment.

CHAPTER 5   Calculation of income tax

1   At what rates is income tax charged on non-savings income?

	✓
10%, 20%, 40% and 50%	
40% and 50%	
20% only	
20%, 40% and 50%	✓

2 Albert's income tax liability is:

£ | 1,479.00

	Non-savings income £	Savings income £	Dividend income £	Total £
Total income	12,000	2,000	3,000	17,000
Less: personal allowance	(8,105)	–	–	(8,105)
Taxable income	3,895	2,000	3,000	8,895

	£
Tax on non-savings income	
£3,895 × 20%	779.00
Tax on savings income	
£2,000 × 20%	400.00
Tax on dividend income	
£3,000 × 10%	300.00
Tax liability	1,479.00

The £3,000 of dividend income falls within the basic rate band so is taxed at 10%.

3 Carol's income tax liability is:

£ | 5,051.12

	Non-savings income £	Savings income £	Dividend income £	Total £
Employment income	4,000			
Interest (× 100/80)		18,000		
Dividends (× 100/90)			22,000	
Total income	4,000	18,000	22,000	44,000
Less: personal allowance	(4,000)	(4,105)		(8,105)
Taxable income	–	13,895	22,000	35,895

	£
Tax on savings income	
£2,710 × 10%	271.00
£11,185 × 20%	2,237.00
£13,895	
Tax on dividend income	
£20,475 × 10%	2,047.50
£1,525 × 32.5%	495.62
£22,000	
Income tax liability	5,051.12

4 Harry's income tax liability is:

£ | 70,876.00

	Non-savings income £	Savings income £	Dividend income £	Total £
Employment income	140,000			
Interest (× 100/80)		20,000		
Dividends (× 100/90)			30,000	
Total income	140,000	20,000	30,000	190,000
Less: personal allowance	(Nil)			(Nil)
Taxable income	140,000	20,000	30,000	190,000

	£
Tax on non-savings income	
£34,370 × 20%	6,874.00
£105,630 × 40%	42,252.00
£140,000	
Tax on savings income	
£10,000 × 40%	4,000.00
£10,000 × 50%	5,000.00
£20,000	
Tax on dividend income	
£30,000 × 42.5%	12,750.00
Income tax liability	70,876.00

5 Basic rate tax relief is obtained by paying Gift Aid donations net of 20% tax. Further tax relief is given to higher and additional rate taxpayers by extending the basic rate band by the gross amount of the Gift Aid donation.

6

	Non-savings income £	Savings income £	Dividend income £	Total £
Pension income	17,000			
Property income	3,500			
Interest (received gross)		380		
Dividends (× 100/90)			700	
Total income	20,500	380	700	21,580
Less: personal allowance	(10,660)			(10,660)
Taxable income	9,840	380	700	10,920

Premium bond prizes are exempt from income tax.

	£
Tax on non-savings income	
£9,840 × 20%	1,968.00
Tax on savings income	
£380 × 20%	76.00
Tax on dividend income	
£700 × 10%	70.00
	2,114.00
Less: tax suffered at source	
tax credit on dividends	(70.00)
tax deducted from pension income	(2,010.00)
Tax payable	34.00

7

	Non-savings income £	Savings income £	Dividend income £	Total £
Business profits	37,000			
Building society interest				
(× 100/80)		5,000		
Dividends (× 100/90)			4,000	
Total income	37,000	5,000	4,000	46,000
Less: personal allowance	(8,105)			(8,105)
Taxable income	28,895	5,000	4,000	37,895

Tax on non-savings income	£
£28,895 × 20%	5,779.00
Tax on savings income	
£5,000 × 20%	1,000.00
Tax on dividend income	
£475 × 10%	47.50
£2,000 (extended) × 10%	200.00
£1,525 × 32.5%	495.62
Income tax liability	7,522.12
Less: tax credit on dividends	(400.00)
tax suffered on interest	(1,000.00)
Tax payable	6,122.12

8

	✓
£49,370	
£34,370	
£46,370	
£53,120	✓

(£15,000 x 100/80 = £18,750 + £34,370)

CHAPTER 6   Self-assessment of income tax

1   The due filing date for an income tax return for 2012/13 assuming the taxpayer will submit the return online is:

| 31 January 2014 |

2   The 2012/13 payments on account will be calculated as

| 50% |

of the income tax payable for

| 2011/12 |

and will be due on

| 31 January 2013 |

and

| 31 July 2013 |

3 £100 penalty for failure to deliver return on time.

Possible £10 per day penalty from 1 May 2014 until date of filing.

5% penalty on tax paid late. Interest on tax paid late.

4

	✓
31 January 2015	
31 March 2015	
6 April 2015	
28 January 2015	✓

A year after the actual filing date because Sase filed the return before the due filing date (31 January 2014).

5 Jamie's 2012/13 payments on account will each be

£	6,000

and will be due on

31 January 2013

and

31 July 2013

Jamie's balancing payment will be

£	4,000

and will be due on

31 January 2014

6

£	0

No penalties for late payment are due on late payments on account.

7   Identify the maximum penalty that could be imposed on her.

	✓
£5,100	
£3,400	
£1,020	✓
£2,380	

30% × PLR

PLR = £17,000 × 20% = £3,400

CHAPTER 7   Computing capital gains tax

1   Which of the following constitute chargeable disposals for CGT?

	Chargeable ✓	Exempt ✓
A gift of an antique necklace	✓	
The sale of a building	✓	

2   Her chargeable gain on sale is:

£ | 235,000

	£
Proceeds	560,000
Less: cost	(325,000)
Chargeable gain	235,000

3

The chargeable gain/allowable loss arising is:

	✓
£16,663	✓
£17,500	
£19,663	
£18,337	

	£
Proceeds	38,000
Less: costs of disposal	(3,000)
	35,000
Less: £41,500 × $\dfrac{38,000}{38,000 + 48,000}$	(18,337)
Chargeable gain	16,663

4 The amount is liable to CGT in 2012/13 is:

> £ | 145,100

The losses carried forward are:

> £ | 0

	£
Gains	171,000
Less: current year losses	(5,300)
	165,700
Less: losses b/f	(10,000)
	155,700
Less: annual exempt amount	(10,600)
Taxable gains	145,100

5

Calculate Martha's CGT liability for 2012/13, assuming she is a higher rate taxpayer and made chargeable gains (before the annual exempt amount) of £23,800 in October 2012.

> £ | 3,696

	£
Chargeable gains	23,800
Less: annual exempt amount	(10,600)
Taxable gains	13,200
CGT on £13,200 @ 28%	3,696

6

A loss arising on a disposal to a connected person can be set against any gains arising in the same year or in subsequent years.

	✓
True	
False	✓

A loss on a disposal to a connected person can be set only against gains arising on disposals to the same connected person.

7   No gain or loss arises on a disposal to a spouse/civil partner.

	✓
True	✓
False	

8

	Actual proceeds used	Deemed proceeds (market value) used	No gain or loss basis
Paul sells an asset to his civil partner Joe for £3,600			✓
Grandmother gives an asset to her grandchild worth £1,000		✓	
Sarah sells an asset to best friend Cathy for £12,000 worth £20,000		✓	

CHAPTER 8   Chattels and private residences

1   The gain arising if he sells it for:

(a)   £5,800 after deducting selling expenses of £180 is:

£	Nil

There is no gain as the chattel is sold for gross proceeds of less than £6,000.

(b)   £8,200 after deducting selling expenses of £220 is:

£	4,033

	£
Net proceeds	8,200
Less: cost	(3,500)
	4,700

Gain cannot exceed 5/3 (8,420 – 6,000) = £4,033
Therefore, gain is £4,033

2 The gain arising is:

£	Nil

A racehorse is an exempt asset as it is a wasting chattel, so no chargeable gain or allowable loss arises.

3 The loss arising is:

£	(1,000)

	£
Deemed proceeds	6,000
Less: cost	(7,000)
Allowable loss	(1,000)

4 Provided the property has at some time been the owner's principal private residence, the last .... months of ownership is always an exempt period.

How many months?

	✓
12	
24	
36	✓
48	

5 Providing the taxpayer actually occupies the property both before and at some point after the period of absence, the following periods are deemed to be occupied for the purpose of PPR exemption:

(a) Periods of up to three years for any reason. Where a period of absence exceeds three years, three years out of the longer period are deemed to be a period of occupation.

(b) Periods during which the owner was required by his employment to live abroad.

(c) Period of up to four years where the owner was:

  (i) Self-employed and forced to work away from home (UK and abroad);

  (ii) Employed and required to work elsewhere in the UK (overseas employment is covered by (b) above).

6   Using the proforma below compute the gain on sale.

	£
Proceeds	180,000
Cost	(60,000)
Gain before PPR exemption	120,000
PPR exemption 145/212 × £120,000	(82,075)
Gain	37,925

Principal private residence exemption

	Exempt months	Chargeable months
1 April 1995 to 31 July 1998 (actual occupation)	40	
1 August 1998 to 31 July 2002 (employed abroad)	48	
1 August 2002 to 30 April 2004 (actual occupation)	21	
1 May 2004 to 30 November 2009		67
1 December 2009 to 30 November 2012 (last 36 months)	36	—
	145	67

Exempt 145/212 × £120,000 = £82,075

7

	✓
22/25	
14/25	
17/25	✓
19/25	

The 5 years posted abroad will not be included as he never returned to the property. Therefore only the actual 14 years of occupation and the last 36 months will be included.

CHAPTER 9   Shares

1   Her chargeable gain is:

	✓
£9,000	
£11,500	
£17,000	
£14,250	✓

	No. of shares	Cost
	£	£
August 1992 Acquisition	10,000	5,000
April 2007 Acquisition	10,000	16,000
	20,000	21,000
November 2012 Disposal	(15,000)	(15,750)
c/f	5,000	5,250

	£
Proceeds of sale	30,000
Less: allowable cost	(15,750)
Chargeable gain	14,250

2

	✓
True	
False	✓

In a rights issue, shares are paid for and this amount is added to the original cost. In a bonus issue, shares are not paid for and so there is no adjustment to the original cost.

3 His chargeable gain is:

£	3,750

No. of shares		*Cost*
		£
May 2001 Acquisition	2,000	12,000
December 2002 1 for 2 rights issue @ £7.50	1,000	7,500
	3,000	19,500
March 2013 Disposal	(2,500)	(16,250)
c/f	500	3,250

	£
Proceeds of sale	20,000
Less: allowable costs	(16,250)
Chargeable gain	3,750

4 Her chargeable gain is:

£	7,000

	No. of shares	*Cost*
		£
June 2009 Acquisition	6,000	15,000
August 2010 1 for 3 bonus issue	2,000	nil
	8,000	15,000
December 2012 Disposal	(8,000)	(15,000)
c/f	nil	nil

	£
Proceeds of sale	22,000
Less: allowable costs	(15,000)
Chargeable gain	7,000

INDEX

Notes

REVIEW FORM

How have you used this Text?
(Tick one box only)

☐ Home study

☐ On a course _____

☐ Other _____

Why did you decide to purchase this Text? *(Tick one box only)*

☐ Have used BPP Texts in the past

☐ Recommendation by friend/colleague

☐ Recommendation by a college lecturer

☐ Saw advertising

☐ Other _____

During the past six months do you recall seeing/receiving either of the following?
(Tick as many boxes as are relevant)

☐ Our advertisement in Accounting Technician

☐ Our Publishing Catalogue

Which (if any) aspects of our advertising do you think are useful?
(Tick as many boxes as are relevant)

☐ Prices and publication dates of new editions

☐ Information on Text content

☐ Details of our free online offering

☐ None of the above

Your ratings, comments and suggestions would be appreciated on the following areas of this Text.

	Very useful	Useful	Not useful
Introductory section	☐	☐	☐
Quality of explanations	☐	☐	☐
How it works	☐	☐	☐
Chapter tasks	☐	☐	☐
Chapter Overviews	☐	☐	☐
Test your learning	☐	☐	☐
Index	☐	☐	☐

	Excellent	Good	Adequate	Poor
Overall opinion of this Text	☐	☐	☐	☐

Do you intend to continue using BPP Products? ☐ Yes   ☐ No

Please note any further comments and suggestions/errors on the reverse of this page. The author of this edition can be e-mailed at:
ambercottrell@bpp.com

Please return to: Amber Cottrell, Tax Publishing Manager, BPP Learning Media Ltd, FREEPOST, London, W12 8BR.

REVIEW FORM (continued)

TELL US WHAT YOU THINK

Please note any further comments and suggestions/errors below.